30 Days of Spiritual Detox

Healing for the Hardened, Hurried, and

Harassed Heart

Donald M Bell Sr

ISBN: 150010132X
ISBN 13: 9781500101329

Cover Design and Layout: [Donald M. Bell Sr.]. Editing: Mary C. Lewis, MCL Editing, etc.

To Mary Frances Bell-Bagby, who taught me how to listen;
William Elmo Bagby, who taught me how to communicate;
David Samuel Bell, who taught me how to learn;
Pastor Kenneth C. Ulmer and Pastor Felton Simpson, who taught me about faith;
Charles Brooks, who taught me about hope;
My wife and kids, who taught me about love; and
The Father, Son, and Holy Spirit, who continue to teach me.

Contents

Foreword

The testimony that God gives of a man named David is one of the greatest testimonies of man in all scripture. In Acts 13:22, the Lord said, "I have found King David, son of Jesse, a man after my own heart; he will do everything I want him to do" (NIV). And yet this same King David prayed to the Lord, "Create in me a clean heart" (Psalm 51:10 NIV). In 1 Samuel 10:9, the Spirit of the Lord moved on a man named King Saul and the Lord gave him another heart. The heart is at the core of your being.

Salvation is an issue of the heart. "If you confess with your mouth... and believe in your heart...you will be saved" (Romans 10:9 NIV). You are as you think in your heart: "For as he thinks in his heart, so is he" (Proverbs 23:7 NKJV). A popular gospel song paraphrases David's prayer with the musical petition, "Give me a clean heart; so I may follow thee" (*A Clean Heart*, 1970, Dr. Margaret Douroux). Jesus declares His blessing on those who have a clean heart and promises the revelation of the presence of God: "Blessed are the pure in heart, for they shall see God" (Matthew 5:8 KJV). A life lived in relationship with the Living God is always concerned with the condition of the heart.

Victory and success in the life of the Christian are always related to the purity of the heart. Holiness is not merely about what is in your head or on your note pad or what you write in the margins of your Bible. The psalmist says, "I have hidden your word in my heart that I might not sin against you" (Psalm 119:11 NIV). There is a spiritual relationship between growing in the Word and growing in the Lord.

One of the most challenging disciplines facing the person who desires to grow in their relationship with Jesus the Christ is dedicated time with the Word of God. In our fast-food, microwave world of tweets, texts, and the like, the priority of investigation, meditation, and application of the eternal truths of God's Word slowly but surely drifts to the bottom of our to-do lists. However, it is spiritually impossible to maintain a healthy spiritual life without a regular diet of the Word of God.

The additional challenge in achieving this goal of successful spiritual maturity is to find a tool that is both substantive and simplistic: one that contains enough spiritual truth that your requirement of "daily bread" is met but that does not choke you in the process. God has used Pastor Donald Bell to produce a discipleship tool that is both substantive and simplistic. Firmly rooted and grounded in biblical revelation, each daily experience with the Word will give you a scriptural principle. However, Pastor Bell does not stop with a neatly packaged formula of five steps to do *this* or seven insights into *that*. In the very palatable, digestible, practical manner that characterizes his teaching gift, he presents the critical element of simple application. Of course, simple is sometimes challenging. Simple is sometimes difficult. Simple is sometimes uncomfortable, and yet this work will lovingly move you from theory to practice, from belief to behavior, and from glory to glory as the Holy Spirit patiently conforms you to the image of the Son of God.

This journey will cost you time. It will cost you commitment. It will cost you consistency. But the rewards, the benefit, and the harvest that God will produce is a fresh passion for godly things as He pumps life through you and restores your heart, revives your spirit, and renews your mind. You will never be the same.

Pastor Kenneth C. Ulmer
Senior Pastor-Teacher
Faithful Central Bible Church
Los Angeles, California

Introduction

Keep your heart with all vigilance, for
from it flow the springs of life.
—*Proverbs 4:23*

Heart disease has been given the name the "silent killer" because one-third of the people with heart disease don't know they have the disease and because it takes a couple of decades for the average person with heart disease to develop symptoms. So many cases go undiagnosed and untreated that many people with heart ailments are unaware that a silent assassin stalks them. As part of the effort to address the epidemic of heart disease, governments and aid organizations spend millions of dollars a year on public service announcements designed to encourage people to take care of their hearts by eating a proper diet, getting exercise, and having regular checkups.

Because of the efforts of government and private agencies like the National Heart and Lung Institute Foundation, a large number of Americans are aware of the steps they can take to prevent heart disease, and, what's more, they have begun to incorporate them into their lifestyles. Despite the countless amount of time and energy devoted to raising awareness about heart care in the physical realm, relatively little has been done to promote heart health awareness in the spiritual realm, even though the same level of risk exists in the spiritual realm as in the physical realm. In the same way that a lifestyle of neglect and disregard for the health of the physical heart can have a crippling effect on our overall physical health, a lifestyle of neglect and disregard for spiritual heart health can have an equally devastating effect on our overall spiritual health. For years we may take part in so-called spiritual activities, unaware of the early warning signs of a spiritually compromised heart. When we let our lives settle into a routine so overwhelming (abused) and/or monotonous (neglected) that it becomes impossible to engage life with a level of mindfulness and authenticity that permits us to do little more than exist, the stage has been set for "spiritual heart failure."

Spiritual heart failure can occur in the life of the most accomplished believer. Even someone as accomplished as King Solomon, who was raised by a father who was called "a man after (God's) own heart" (Acts 13:22), can have his or her life and legacy marred by spiritual heart failure. Although King Solomon amassed an astonishing degree of wealth; reigned over Israel during an extended season of peace and prosperity; counseled luminaries from around the world; composed 3,000 proverbs and 1,005 songs; authored three books of the Bible (Song of Songs, Ecclesiastes, and Proverbs); and built a temple to the Lord so magnificent that Jews still pray three times a day for its restoration, King Solomon's reign came to a tragic end when God made it clear he was suffering from spiritual heart failure. In chapter 11 of 1 Kings, God diagnosed King Solomon with a severe case of spiritual heart failure caused by gradually turning his heart away from the Lord, which drew a comparison to the heart of his father, King David, whose heart was wholly turned to the Lord (1 Kings 11:1–9). The story of King Solomon's life is a cautionary tale about the high cost paid by those who display a lack of appreciation for the role the heart plays in determining the arc of our spiritual development.

Like many well-meaning believers of our time, King Solomon was so consumed by the cares of this world that his heart eventually hardened toward the things of God. King Solomon's reign was terminated by the same progressive disease Christ diagnosed the church at Ephesus with in Revelation 2:1–7: the turning away or abandonment of the heart from what ought to be our first love. Spiritual heart failure can occur in the individual as well as in a spiritual community, such as a congregation or a marriage. Both King Solomon and the Ephesians routinely participated in spiritual practices that should have brought them closer to the Lord, yet they turned their hearts away from the Lord. Both Solomon and the Ephesians lived lives full of obligations and rituals—alienated from God, void of spirit because they stopped encountering God at the heart level.

Ultimately it wasn't King Solomon's love for foreign women that brought him down; he could have survived that in the same way his father did. King Solomon's greatest failure was not addressing the life-threatening sclerosis (hardening of tissue) working its way through his heart while he merrily went about his business.

A Man after God's Own Heart

To gain a deeper understanding of the serious role the heart plays in laying our spiritual foundation, let's examine the life of King Solomon's father, King David, whose heart was said to be wholly turned to the Lord despite a series of personal and public setbacks: coveting, adultery, murder, and treason to name a few (1 Kings 11:4). To maintain his spiritual health and endure all the personal setbacks in his life, King David did what neither the king who reigned before him (King Saul) nor the king that reigned after him (King Solomon, his son) did—*he guarded his heart!*

The best place to start our examination of the life of King David is Psalm 51, a personal prayer penned by King David that arose out of the conviction he felt about an affair he had with the wife (Bathsheba) of one of his generals (Uriah the Hittite), whose death King David orchestrated to cover up the affair. A study of Psalm 51 reveals the level of vigilance, effort, and intentionality it takes to be a person who wholeheartedly pursues God.

Throughout the psalm, King David addresses the core issues in his life that led to the scandal, not the symptoms: the coveting, adultery, and murder. In the opening stanza (vv. 1–6), King David makes it clear that a fraudulent lifestyle and a corrupt heart go hand in hand with one another (v. 1, 2). Instead of merely asking the Lord to forgive him for coveting another man's wife, for murder, and for a whole host of other sins, King David asks the Lord to address the corruption in his heart, which he declares has afflicted him since his birth (v. 5). David closes the first stanza with a contrasting portrait of this state and the condition God desires the heart be kept in, which is to delight in the truth in his inner being (heart), having been taught wisdom in the hidden places of his heart (v. 6).

In the second stanza, King David asks the Lord to take the action that he believes will heal his spiritually compromised heart. The first action King David asks the Lord to take is to purge his heart (v. 7). Prolonged success has a tendency to fill the heart with a stagnant reservoir of pride; in the same manner, prolonged disappointment fills the heart with a stagnant reservoir of shame—which, in either case, needs to be expelled from the heart of the believer. Once purged, the heart needs to be cleansed, which is the next thing King David asks the Lord to do to heal his heart (vv. 8–10). Simply purging the heart is not enough to heal the spiritually compromised heart. It needs to be cleansed before the Lord can perform the third action King David knew he was in need of, which was to fill it. In verses 11–15, David asks the Lord to fill his heart with a fresh stream of willingness, joy, gladness, and praise. King David was wise enough to know that before this filling could take place, God needed to remove the residue of pride and shame that would recontaminate his heart.

The final act of restoration King David asks the Lord to perform regarding his brokenness was a rather odd request, considering the circumstances (vv. 16–17). The last thing you would imagine a person in a downward spiral of shame would want was the very thing King David knew he needed. To truly experience the full restoration of God, our hearts must be broken before the Lord. Brokenness refers to a state of humility brought by the Holy Spirit when we confront the lack of authenticity and out-and-out fraud in our lives with God's standard of righteousness, accompanied by grace and mercy. The purpose of brokenness is to sensitize us to the primary work of the Holy Spirit, which Christ declared was to guide us into all truth (John 16:13). The purpose of our journey toward truth is to confront the natural state of the heart, which scripture declares is "deceitful above all things," "desperately sick," and impossible to know apart from God searching it (Jeremiah 17:9–10). A broken heart is one God is constantly filling with grace and mercy that leaks out through the cracks in our humanity.

After King David finished asking the Lord to restore him, he makes the one request I believe earned him the distinction of being called a man after God's own heart. David's petition, "*Cast me not away from your presence, and take not your Holy Spirit from me*" (Psalm 51:11, emphasis added), demonstrated an understanding of the Holy Spirit not **found anywhere else in the Old Testament and rarely seen in the New Testament, even among the disciples.** King David's grasp of the role the Holy Spirit plays in the spiritual health of the individual is second only to Jesus Christ, who told the disciples it was better that He leave them so the Holy Spirit would come. Before John recorded Christ's teaching on the coming of the Holy Spirit, King David understood the necessity of the abiding presence of the Spirit of God in the life of the believer in a way none of his contemporaries had grasped. If you are to walk with the Lord at the level King David did, the Spirit must abide in and with you—not just come upon you in certain situations and conditions, as was the commonly held belief of his day. For the Spirit of God to abide with and in him, King David realized he needed to be vigilant about the state and condition of his heart. Having served under a king (Saul) who the Spirit departed from, King David understood the necessity of the abiding presence of God at a level few could appreciate, which is why he asked the Lord in Psalm 51 and in other places to run diagnostics on his heart (Psalm 7:8–9; 11:5; 26:2; 139).

Even on his deathbed, King David charged his son, King Solomon, to serve God with "a whole heart and a willing mind," and warned him that the Lord is in the business of knowing what's going on in the heart of everyone (1 Chronicles 28:9). King David's council was so spot-on that when the Lord appeared to King Solomon (1 Kings 9:4–9) at the consecration of the temple, the Lord reaffirmed the charge King David gave King Solomon almost word for word:

> And as for you, if you will walk before me, as King David
> your father walked, with integrity of heart and upright-
> ness, doing according to all that I have commanded
> you, and keeping my statutes and my rules, then I
> will establish your royal throne over Israel forever, as
> I promised King David your father, saying, "You shall

not lack a man on the throne of Israel." But if you turn aside from following me, you or your children, and do not keep my commandments and my statutes that I have set before you, but go and serve other gods and worship them, then I will cut off Israel from the land that I have given them, and the house that I have consecrated for my name I will cast out of my sight, and Israel will become a proverb and a byword among all peoples. And this house will become a heap of ruins. Everyone passing by it will be astonished and will hiss, and they will say, "Why has the LORD done thus to this land and to this house?" Then they will say, "Because they abandoned the LORD their God who brought their fathers out of the land of Egypt and laid hold on other gods and worshiped them and served them. Therefore the LORD has brought all this disaster on them."

In the same way the charge given to King Solomon previously by his father, King David, focused on the heart, the Lord's charge also focused on the care and maintenance of his heart, which is something we know in hindsight he did not take anywhere near as seriously as his father, King David, did. What the American Heart Association tries to convey in the physical realm—take care of your heart in order to maintain your health in furtherance of an enhanced quality of life—King David and the Lord tried to convey to King Solomon in the spiritual realm. The approach King David and King Solomon took to manage their hearts determined the outcome of their lives and their spiritual legacies. King David's consistent concern for the care and maintenance of his heart distinguished him from the splendor and stature of his predecessor, King Saul, and the wealth and wisdom of his son, King Solomon. It was King David's wholehearted, authentic, and passionate pursuit of the Lord that earned him the title conferred on him by God: "a man after (God's) own heart" (1 Samuel 13:14; Acts 13:22).

To achieve such an honor and become a man or woman after God's own heart, we must be guided by the wisdom of Proverbs 4:23 (emphasis added): "*Keep your heart with all vigilance, for from it flow the springs of life."* In the same way the physical heart is kept healthy by a combination of changes in our lifestyle, so too is our spiritual heart. With relatively few changes to our lifestyle, it is possible for any believer to start living a more heartful life, like David. One of the most daunting tasks in this process is figuring out where to start. The answer to **the question of where to start is always with a small lifestyle change you can manage that lets you enjoy a measure of success you can build on.**

It is to that end that I developed the resource you hold in your hand. I wrote *30 Days of Spiritual Detox* for the person who finds him – or herself hardened, hurried, and harassed by the ever quickening pace of modern life. I designed it to help you reengage life at the heart level, which I prayerfully intend would not add to the performance pressure you fold into the process, if you are like me, when you take on something new. For next thirty days, I invite you to engage in the activity prescribed in Proverbs 4:23: *keeping your heart with all vigilance* in order to tap into the true spring of life - The transforming flow of the Spirit.

The Process

Each day, I will present you with a single topic of the heart. Each topic will focus on a single spiritual discipline associated with the care and management of the heart. Each topic serves as a primer for the searching of your heart by raising the awareness of what's going on in your heart through commentary, scripture, prayer, and meditation. The goal for each day is to take a purposeful look at yourself, your circumstances, and your relationship with God at the heart level. Because we live in such a fast-paced, fragmented world, it is possible for us to spend our entire day reacting to our environment from the time we get out of bed to the time we lay down without ever engaging our heart. Living in a highly adrenalized state of arousal that encourages quick reactions over authentic communication eventually devolves into a life besieged by meaningless ritual. To break the cycle and overcome the flat-line state that many of our hearts periodically drift into, God has to pull out the spiritual paddles to jump-start our hearts.

Don't be surprised if the topic of the day unearths another issue. Heart work is like participating in an archeological dig; most of it focuses on removing layers of debris. The more layers removed, the more discoveries the process yields. Do not worry about trying to get at everything in one day; when the next day comes, go ahead and move on to the next topic. Remember, one of the goals of the process is to develop the spiritual discipline that will enable you to revisit whatever comes up over the course of your life. Right now, the goal is building awareness and discipline, not addressing issues. Trust me; that will come later. Through consistent practice, you'll be training yourself to live one day at a time (cliché, I know), in the moment, in what Paul describes in Romans 1:17 as "from faith to faith," which means acting in faith today that builds the faith we will need to act in faith tomorrow. At the end of the thirty days, if there is an issue you need to address, feel free to go back over any topic that stood out to you. You can take a week or month or as long as it takes to process whatever comes up. You may also decide to pick a few topics to work on for the entire year. Let the Spirit lead you; the choice is yours. I designed *30 Days of Spiritual Detox* to help you build discipline while you are on a journey.

One of the things I have learned from the feedback of those who have gone through thirty days of spiritual detox is that taking an honest look at yourself can be a very enlightening process. I have also learned that it can be a very painful process as well, especially when people get stuck focusing on the thoughts and conclusions they have drawn about themselves that they find troubling. Should that happen to you, as it does with most, just make a note of it on a blank sheet of paper in the journal or notebook you are using to document your journey, and don't beat yourself up over it. If it happens again, make a note of it right under the previous issue you found disturbing. Do not highlight, capitalize, underline, number, circle, or mark any item on your list in a manner that would distinguish one item from another. Also, do not reread, rehearse, count, or share your list with anyone, including group members. I promise we will deal with the entire list before the end of the book. At first, all I want you to do is write down whatever you find troubling and keep it moving. The only time you need to look at this page is when you are writing down something that troubles you.

Every week starts with an introduction of a theme that ties together the heart topics for that week. Each theme draws on a metaphor taken from the treatment of heart disease. Because each topic of the heart is to be read in the morning, once a week you will need to set aside some time in the evening, preferably not right before you go to bed, to read the introduction for the upcoming week to stay on track.

Suggested Flow

While people have benefitted a great deal from going through *30 Days of Spiritual Detox* on their own, the greatest self-results people have reported to me have been achieved in a small group setting of no more than six, followed by success among husbands and wives. If you are going through *30 Days of Spiritual Detox* with a group or as a couple, it's about a six-week process.

Preparation for Week One:

Identify the group facilitator before the first meeting. Distribute the books at least a week in advance. Have everyone read the "Introduction," "The Process," "A Word of Caution," and "It's a Detox" sections before the first meeting.

Week One:

Use week one to handle all of the logistics surrounding group dynamics and participation (meeting dates, time, duration, location, etc.). Go over all the pre-reading assignments, answering any questions the participants may have at this time. Make sure everyone has a clear grasp of all the points raised in the section titled A Word of Caution. Whoever is facilitating the group should emphasize the seriousness of each topic, making sure to get a verbal commitment from everyone in the group to abide by all the protocols and guidelines spelled out in the book as well as those unique to the group as spelled out by the group facilitator. The facilitator should present all the guidelines and protocols in writing, with a copy given to each participant for their record and review as needed.

Weeks Two through Five Gatherings:

The objective of these meetings are to do a once-a-week check-in with every member of the group to see where they are in the process and for them to share what the process is yielding—in a nonjudgmental atmosphere, which includes extreme self-criticism on the part of a group member while sharing about themselves. Because of the number of areas we will be touching on each week, it is important that someone monitor the time closely so everyone shares, no matter how introverted or shy he or she is. Wisdom has taught me that the ones who share last one week should probably start the sharing the next week to balance things out. During the sharing time, everyone should share one or two things that stood out to him or her that week and why. Close every gathering with prayer driven by compassion.

Week Five: Homework Assignment

At some point after day twenty-eight is completed but before the week-six gathering, members need to pull out their lists of troubling thoughts and conclusions they have drawn about themselves, reduce the list to one item that captures the theme of what troubles them, and write it at the bottom of the paper. After that, they should draw a line through all the other items on the list; those things are merely the symptoms. The theme is the diagnosis. The only thing they should be focused on in moving forward is the diagnosis, not the symptoms. The reason for this is that the heart does not do well trying to address a bunch of issues at one time. Christ was right when he said it is impossible to serve more than one master.

Week-Six Gathering:

The objective of the week-six meeting is to do the final check-in with each member of the group. In this gathering, the facilitator will call upon each member to give a brief summary of his or her takeaway from the group. Included in the summaries should be the diagnosis members plan to work on moving forward. Members should also state what they plan to do next to sustain their spiritual momentum. They should also share a future date they have chosen to go back through *30 Days of Spiritual Detox* a second time. This is also the time to bring closure to the group, as well as to celebrate one another's faithfulness to each other and the process. Consider the prospect of meeting periodically (e.g., quarterly or semiannually) for a while to encourage each other in this heart-health pursuit.

A Word of Caution

If you are doing thirty days of spiritual detox as a couple or in a group setting, I need to caution you about three things. The first thing is not to judge what your mate or other members of your group share. Remember, the truth is composed of facts and authentic opinions. People's thoughts, opinions, assessments, and conclusions are always true and valid when they are an authentic expression of who and where they are, even if they are factually inaccurate or questionable. The goal of this process is to let people share their discoveries in a safe environment, the same way Christ did with the woman he met at a well on a journey through Samaria (John 4). During their encounter, Christ did not try to fix, heal, rebuke, train, challenge, or get her to understand his point, nor did he try to cast anything out of her. There is enough of that kind of stuff taking place among believers when they gather already. The only thing the other people going through the process with you need from you is your presence. If you hear something you think just has to be corrected, use this opportunity to examine your own need to comment and practice any one of the acts of love identified in 1 Corinthians 13. Recognize that our need to correct others says more about what is going on inside of us than it does about the level of dysfunction and error in the lives of those we need to fix. My second caution involves hyper spiritualization of the process, my personal pet peeve for which I have to practice 1 Corinthians 13. Trust me on this; where two or three are gathered in his name, there will always be someone in the group who is more comfortable with "spiritual principles" and the policing of others than they are with reality and personal reflection. If the group doesn't deal with this early, the entire journey will be hijacked, and the people in the group will be too intimidated to do any authentic sharing. Think of hyper spiritu-alization as a cancer that must be diagnosed and eradicated before it spreads. The third thing I want to warn you against is the 'weap-onizing' of information gathered during sharing time. The *weapon-izing* of information occurs when people take what they have learned during time of sharing and leverage it to their advantage in another circumstance, such as bringing it up in a subsequent conversation to coerce the person who shared it, or divulging what was said in group with a third party, also known as gossip. Whatever you do, don't turn what someone shares with you into something you use against them, no matter how appropriate, true, or necessary you think it is to get them to see something. Again, do not do it! If it is found that someone is engaged in the weaponizing of information shared in a group, he or she should be asked out of the group immediately. Guarding the hearts of the people in your group by creating a safe atmosphere is just as important as following up on your homework assignments and having something to share during your weekly gatherings.

It's a Detox

Just like the first thirty days of any stint in rehab, *30 Days of Spiritual Detox* is only the beginning of the transformation process. You will live with and work on many of these topics for the rest of your life. Embrace the next thirty days as a process—not as an assignment, goal, or event. Keep in mind that the next thirty days are to be experienced and not managed. The real value of the detox aspect of the process is not what it pours into you; it is what it draws out of you.

For the next thirty days, do your best to limit the distractions in your life. As much as possible, try to limit your consumption of elec-tronic media. This might also be a good time to take a break from Facebook, Twitter, and other social sites. Avoid the urge to tweet, text, or post your way through the process. One of the goals of the pro-cess is regaining intimacy with yourself, God, and those who are work-ing through it with you in a group setting. Don't worry; all of your Facebook family and followers will be there when you are done. Seek to unplug yourself from technology as much as is reasonably possible. If you simply have to post something, I would not mind if you post a picture of the cover of the book with a comment saying, "I'm going through spiritual detox; see you in thirty days."

Another thing to keep in mind while you are going through the thirty days is the law of sowing and reaping. You are only going to get out of this what you put into it. Authenticity is essential—if you are not willing to engage each topic in an open and honest, nonjudgmental manner, you are not going to connect with the truth, which King David says the Lord desires it to inhabit your inner being (Psalm 51:6) and Christ said will make you free if it abides in you (John 8:32).

May the Lord bless your obedience and effort to open your heart to His Word, His will, and His way!

Day One

Consistency

(1 Corinthians 13:1–13)

Today's heart topic is consistency. Consistency is the ability to maintain a standard over time without much deviation. Frequently, consistency is portrayed as a luxury item a person should aspire to possess instead of a discipline necessary for survival. People will often make light of the various inconsistent areas in their lives without giving much thought to the cost of that inconsistency. Yet when you think about it, inconsistency can and does have a profound impact on our lives; an inconsistent approach to diet and exercise can develop into a situation that has life or death consequences. Inconsistency in paying bills would have a devastating effect on a person's finances, potentially reaching into the hundreds of thousands of dollars in unnecessary interest payments, which plays a significant role in determining if a person is going to live in poverty or prosperity. Think of the consequences inconsistent parenting has on the well-being and fortunes of families multiple generations out, not to mention the effect it has on communities.

Consistency is not a rare gift handed out by God to a select group of super elite, spiritual high achievers. On the contrary, consistency is an essential part of our day-to-day life in the Spirit. Strengthening the heart to handle the daily demands of life in a consistent manner are the baby steps every believer must take in order to be counted among the faithful. The proverb that asserts the notion, "those who are faithful over a few things will be made rulers over many things" illustrates the profound role consistency plays in a rewarding life.

Trivializing our inconstancies is the same as trivializing the impact God wants us to have on the world. Those who desire a closer walk with the Lord must embrace consistency as a spiritual discipline on par with prayer and fasting. One of the realities the serious believer must come to terms with, if they are going to make a commitment to walk in God's will, is the corresponding commitment they will have to make to walk in consistency. God's will is not something one tries or dabbles in; it is something we must commit to with a heart fortified in consistency.

Consistency is a crucial part of every fruitful endeavor the Lord instructs us to carry out. When Christ instructs His disciples to pray the Lord's Prayer, consistency is a central theme of His teaching. From the beginning, He tells them to do it consistently. The petition "give us this day our daily bread" (Luke 11:3) is an appeal that needs to be made consistently on a daily basis. At the end of Paul's life, the theme of his charge to his young protégé, Timothy, was to be consistent. In 2 Timothy 4:2, he tells the soon-to-be spiritually orphaned Timothy, "Be ready in season and out of season...with complete patience." In 4:3–4, he warns Timothy, "People will not endure sound teaching" and that they "will turn away...and wander." In the face of the inconsistent behavior of others, Paul challenges young Timothy in 4:5 to be consistent: "Always be sober minded, endure suffering...fulfill your ministry." In 4:7, Paul summarizes his charge to Timothy about consistency when he offers his own testimony as an example: "I have fought the good fight, I have finished the race, I have kept the faith." All that lies ahead for him and others, he says, is the reward that the Lord will grant those who discharged their call with consistency.

In 1 Corinthians 13:1–8, where Paul defines love, a number of the elements he uses to describe the true nature of love are synonymous with consistency: love that is "patient" (13:4); "bears all things, believes all things, hopes all things, endures all things" (13:7); and "never ends" (13:8) is love that is consistent. If a major part of the validation of our identity as Disciples of Christ before the world is our love toward one another (John 13:35), then we cannot take consistency lightly. It must be front and center in everything we do. To walk in consistency, our approach and actions toward others must escape the gravitational pull of our fluctuating moods in search of a higher standard than what we feel like doing on any particular day.

As you seek the Lord's heart today, do not just ask Him to make you a more consistent person; also ask Him to show you the cost of your inconsistency to yourself and to others. Ask Him to make you sensitive to the impact of your inconsistency on the ones you love. Spend time meditating on the role consistency plays in the Lord's definition of love in 1 Corinthians 13:1–13.

Day Two

Zeal

(Revelation 2:1–7)

Today's heart topic is zeal. Zeal describes the level of enthusiasm and passion a person approaches life with. The opposite of zeal is complacency, a state of self-satisfaction that makes you vulnerable. It develops in the heart of people whose expectations have lost touch with their blessings, as well as the nature and character of the one who blesses. In Romans 10:2, Paul said the people of Israel had zeal for the Lord "but not according to knowledge." If he were writing a letter addressed to the church in America, Paul might flip that and say we have knowledge and no zeal.

One of the greatest threats to heart-led ministry, according to my pastor, Bishop K.C. Ulmer, is the potential that over time you can get so good at doing it that your heart no longer has to be engaged to get things done. In the early 1980s, Cadillac designed a motor called the V-8-6-4 engine. The engine used eight cylinders to get up to speed, and then it dropped from eight to six and then to four cylinders, once it reached sixty miles per hour. Even though the engine was so ahead of its time, it would take another thirty years for automakers to get it right. The concept was based on sound, scientific principle: it takes more energy to get a car up to sixty miles per hour than it does to run it at that speed. The same laws of inertia that govern the physics of keeping a car running at sixty miles per hour also govern momentum in the spirit realm: once we achieve a state of competency at an endeavor, the less energy it takes to execute. The same law that works for you in the physical realm works against you in the spiritual realm. The reduced energy needed in the spiritual realm equates to less focus and intentionality, which produces a mindset that makes us vulnerable to complacency. This is what occurred at the church in Ephesus. In Revelation 2, Christ told the church their success had fostered an atmosphere of complacency. Even though there was no immorality, scandal, or apostasy in the church, their self-satisfaction still produced a level of complacency resembling the dimensions of an iceberg, with only a portion of it barely breaching the surface, the remainder of its massive bulk remaining submerged.

What made the situation at the church of Ephesus so disturbing was not the state of complacency they were in; it was the fact that they did not know their hearts had drifted away from the Lord. Whenever we arrive at a state of competence where we are consistently able to produce good results, we must be extra vigilant about the state of our hearts. The fire that fueled our success can go out, and we won't even know it. Consider how many times Sampson rose up to fight the Philistines before the time he rose up to fight them and the Spirit of God had left him, with no tangible evidence of his departure other than a new haircut (Judges 16). Just like people on diet and exercise programs must work their way around the weight-loss plateaus they occasionally reach, we must be prepared to move beyond the spiritual plateaus we come across. We can't let success rob us of our passion and enthusiasm.

As you seek the Lord's heart today, ask Him to give you a passion for the things that please Him. Ask the Lord to give you a renewed passion to see His will be done on earth as it is in heaven. Ask the Lord to show you the passions in your life that compete with your 'First Love' (Him). Spend time meditating on the ways people abandon their First Love. Ask the Lord to show you a few of the things that may be hindering you from pursuing Him with all of your heart, all of your soul, and all your might. Ask God to show you if there are any discrepancies between your First Love and your ultimate concern.

Day Three

Sacrifice

(Luke 14:25–33)

Today's topic of the heart is sacrifice. Sacrifice occurs when you give up something that you have a legitimate claim to for the benefit of someone else. A sacrifice is not something you do for someone and wait for him or her to reciprocate—that is called a favor. Favors are things we do for others that obligate them to do something for us at another time. A sacrifice is also not something you do for someone to gain an advantage over him or her; we call that leverage. A true sacrifice is a loss we voluntarily take on without self-regard.

In Christ's teaching on the cost of discipleship (Luke 14:25–33), He identifies five potential areas of impact sacrifice can have on our lives. The first potential cost to our lives that Christ identifies is the potential that a sacrifice may change the dynamics of our relationships. Whenever we feel so strongly about something that we are willing to make sacrifices for it, those closest to us are the ones who may struggle the most with our decision. Because our family and friends want the best for us (from their point of view), it is difficult for them to watch us forego some of the privileges and pleasures life has to offer. People may become afraid, anxious, and even offended by our choices, especially when we make a commitment to something they neither understand nor believe in.

The second area of impact sacrifice may have on our lives is personal. When Christ says a disciple must hate even his or her own life to follow him (v. 26), He is not talking about a lack of self-esteem based on self-loathing; He is describing an essential quality of those who walk in sacrifice effectively, namely humility. Those who approach sacrifice with humility are able to set aside their wants and needs in order to serve a cause beyond the scope of their own self-interest. Instead of devoting their time and resources to the enhancement of their own pleasure, possessions, and position, they do what I call "big picture living." Big picture living places a greater value on the impact that one's actions has on others over time instead of the number of personal achievements they can accomplish.

The third potential way sacrifice may impact your life deals with the level and duration in which you may have to endure. When Christ teaches on bearing your own cross (Matthew 10:38; Luke 9:23–24), He is plainly referring to the pain that must be endured to make a sacrifice. Of all the possible spheres of impact that sacrifice may have on a person's life, perhaps there is none more challenging than the prospect of dealing with pain. To manage psychological pain so that it does not turn into suffering, the heart has to resolve three things: the limitations placed on potential options, the limited number of potential people to provide support, and the unspecified amount of time they may have to devote to the process. Put simply, the resilient must be prepared to live in a season with no out, no end, and no friend.

The fourth potential place of impact is in the area of reason. When Christ instructs us to count the cost before we go off to war or build a tower, He is talking about the role reason plays in making a sacrifice (Luke 14:28–30). Every sacrifice we make is a calculated risk; counting the cost means accepting responsibility for our choices, which means we can't claim we are a victim of someone's deception or abuse. In the same way Christ declared He was not a victim when He said no one could take His life because He was laying it down willingly (John 10:17–18), our sacrifice must reflect our deliberate choice—not the choices of others. The truth is that your action is not a sacrifice if you retain the right to whine, blame, or default on your commitment.

The fifth area where sacrifice potentially impacts us is in the area of loss. When Christ talks of renouncing everything, He is talking about the loss people suffer when they make sacrifices (Luke 14:25–33). When confronted with loss, we are challenged to embrace the hardest work the human heart is fitted to perform: grieving. Grief is all about adjusting to change, which in my opinion is the most difficult thing the human psyche has to process. It involves two acts that are emotionally opposed to one another: the fear and frustration of the death of things we hoped for and the challenge of the birth of opportunity that breeds new hope. After a loss, we are faced with the challenge of processing the end of something as we know it, while at the same time we are facing the beginning of something we may have never known or anticipated. So while we are adjusting to the reality of the fragility of life, simultaneously we must adjust to a new reality with new opportunities. Think of it as sifting through the rubble of a disaster while concurrently needing to develop the blueprints for what we are going to build in its place, taking into account all that we learned in going through the process of losing the previous building.

As you seek the Lord's heart today, ask Him to show you the areas where you are serving him as a favor rather than a loving sacrifice. Ask the Lord to show you the places in your life where you are holding out for a return on your investment in him. Next, broaden your request: ask the Lord to show you the relationships in your life that are based more on favor than love. Spend some time in meditation, counting the cost of your service to the Lord. Look for areas in your life where you have not accepted the cost. Ask the Lord to show you how your perception of your rights need to change and to show you at what level you may need to reprioritize your relationships to reflect your belief that your service to Him and others is a legitimate priority in your life.

Day Four

Hospitality

(Matthew 25:31–46)

Today's topic of the heart is hospitality. Hospitality may be the most biblically spelled out teaching in scripture and perhaps the most neglected of all Christian virtues. In Hebrews 13:2, God commands us to conscientiously show hospitality to strangers. So significant was the duty to show hospitality toward strangers that the writer of Hebrews instructed us to receive every stranger as though he or she were an angel sent by God (Hebrews 23:2). In an age where people are so very self-absorbed, developing a real sensitivity to the comfort and needs of others is difficult, especially when we don't know them or they are significantly different from us and we have been raised in our own narcissistic enclaves of entitlement. Despite our struggle with hospitality in a modern context, it remains a cornerstone of true Christian virtue and the only true path to effective ministry.

In several of Paul's letters (epistles), he expounds on the role hospitality plays in our spiritual lives. In Romans 12, Paul tells the Roman church that hospitality is the mark of genuine Christianity. In 1 Timothy 3:2, Paul says hospitality is one of the traits a man who aspires to be an overseer must have. Later in the book (1 Timothy 5:10), Paul places hospitality among the list of virtues that women with a reputation of godliness possess. To drive home his point about the significance of hospitality in the character of a leader, Paul again places hospitality on the list of qualifications for leadership (1 Timothy 3:2). Peter also proclaimed the importance of hospitality in 1 Peter 4:9 when he instructed believers to show hospitality toward one another, pointing out that charitable acts of hospitality would act as a social lubricant that would cover a multitude of sins.

Even with all the teachings of the prophets and apostles on hospitality, nowhere in scripture is the necessity of hospitality more clearly illustrated than when Christ sent his twelve disciples out to preach the gospel (Matthew 10:5–15). There were two things he instructed them to do that emphasized the importance of hospitality. The first thing he told them to do was not to gather resources for their journey; they were to rely totally on the hospitality of the people in the towns they entered to meet their needs. Secondly, if they came to a house or a town that refused to receive them, they were to leave that town or home and shake the dust from their feet as a sign of judgment, which Christ declared would be worse than Sodom and Gomorrah, a town notorious for wickedness but nonetheless received strangers in their midst. In telling them not to preach in towns and homes where there was no hospitality, Christ was condemning that town or home to eternal judgment because of a failure to show hospitality to strangers. It is a sobering thought to think God would condemn a place for not showing hospitality. The presence or absence of warmth and friendliness in the heart of a person is such an essential component of God's plan for redemption that it determined the eternal disposition of entire towns and homes.

In Matthew 25:31–46, Christ tells His disciples that one of His criteria for judging people will be hospitality. Feeding, clothing, visiting, and welcoming the stranger in a time of need was just as honorable an act as ministering to the Lord Himself; on the other hand, neglecting the call to show hospitality to the needs of the stranger was worthy of eternal punishment.

As you seek the Lord's heart today, ask Him to show you Himself in every stranger that you meet from now on. Ask Him to deliver you from any trauma, prejudice, or apathy that would have you ignore, look past, or mishandle anyone. Ask Him to give you a warm, welcoming spirit for those who live on the fringes. Meditate on the way the Lord would judge you today based on your hospitality toward strangers as described in Matthew 25:31–46. Ask the Lord to show you how to honor and receive those you do not understand.

Day Five

Diligence

(Proverbs 4:20–27)

Today's topic of the heart is diligence. Diligence is hard work executed with care and precision. Simply put, it is work well done. One of the more difficult things to manage when something we want to do taxes us is the accompanying frustration that grows with fatigue. When fatigue sets in, compromise is not far beyond. Most kids know if their parents get tired, they have a better chance at getting what they want because tired minds struggle to keep, enforce, and aspire to high standards.

Whenever we walk faithfully with the Lord for an extended period of time, we will eventually go through a season where the level of excellence we are accustomed to becomes too difficult to sustain. It is in these seasons of weariness that questions about the value of holding to the standard and the prospect of compromise starts to work its way into the heart; a faithful worker who has grown weary may question the sensibility of keeping standards they have set for themselves when others appear to be prospering without a standard. A single woman who is tired of waiting for a mate may revisit the idea of rekindling an old relationship that was dysfunctional. And a young person may question the level of discipline they have been walking in under the pressure from their peers who are living in compromise.

One of the paradoxical qualities of diligence is its ability to play a role in our greatest victories and our greatest temptations. Think about the timing of the devil's confrontation with Christ in the wilderness; the tempter showed up to exploit the undoubted weariness of Christ after forty days of fasting. What the tempter sought to do was invalidate the forty days of fasting by getting him to doubt the effect and value of his efforts. It has always been the strategy of the enemy to raise questions about our value to God. This is especially true when we have gone a long time putting forth maximum effort with seemingly minimal results.

After devoting an entire chapter to faith, the writer of Hebrews warns us, not to grow weary or fainthearted in our struggles because God disciplines the ones he loves (Hebrews 12:1–15). In 2 Thessalonians 3:13, Paul encouraged the Thessalonians, whose faith and love he had bragged about to other churches, saying, "Do not grow weary in doing good." The reason Paul encouraged them to remain diligent was to counter the doubts and fears that were setting in due to the constant persecution the church had been under.

As you seek the Lord's heart today, ask Him to give you a deeper care and concern for the long-term effect of your choices. In addition, ask Him to give you the wisdom to know when to rest, ask for help, or let it go. One of the greatest manifestations of human pride is the belief in our own indispensable invulnerability. Ask the Lord to show you where pride is hindering your effectiveness and your ability to work cooperatively with others. Ask the Lord to show you the value of trusting his grace rather than your competence. Meditate on the role that protecting the heart plays in determining the quality and standard of the outcome of your efforts. Ask the Lord to help you make a greater connection between your success and the condition of your heart rather than your success and your credentials.

Day Six

Attitude

(James 3:13–18)

Today's topic of the heart is attitude. Attitude is one of those words that everyone understands but struggles to define, so here goes my contribution. Attitude is the approach or stances we take in a given circumstance based on what we already believe are the entitlements and obligations of others toward us and us toward them. It means this: we handle the people and circumstances out of entitlement and obligation. To put it in more blunt terms, attitude is the way we handle people based on our perception of their worth verses ours.

Attitude is a major theme in scripture as well as a major subtext of other topics. The whole notion of rebellion could be summarized in one phrase: "bad attitude." The whole notion of hope could be summarized as a "positive attitude." Faith could be summarized as a "good attitude." The point is that every spiritual endeavor we undertake has an aspect of it driven by attitude. One of the constant drumbeats of scripture is the admonition to maintain the right attitude. According to scripture, several things can influence our attitude.

One the most obvious forces that influence our attitude is the culture we grow up in. In Romans 12, Paul warns us not to let the world squeeze us into a mold that leads us to think more highly of ourselves than we should. In 1 John 2:15–17, John says it is the love of the world that stimulates emptiness and pride. In 1 Peter 4:1–3, Peter challenges us to arm ourselves with the attitude of Christ to counter the influence of the culture we live in. In 1 Corinthians 7:25–35, Paul talks about the effect that cultural attitudes about marriage have on people's attitude about God—even within the church.

Another force that exerts influence on our attitude is spiritual. When the Spirit of the Lord departed from King Saul and was replaced by a harmful spirit, King Saul experienced such a dramatic change in temperament the men in his court advised him to bring a then young David in his service to play the lyre (string instrument) to soothe him when the harmful spirit afflicted his mood (1 Samuel 16:14-23). On one of Christ's journeys, He met a man who was so tormented by demonic spirits that he was extremely violent (Matthew 8:28–29). The book of Job tells us that the devil is working behind the scenes to derail Job's faith in God. On more than one occasion, Christ attributed the attitude of the people he was dealing with to satanic influences (Matthew 16:23; 23:13–36; John 8:44). It was the influence of a demonic spirit that changed Judas' attitude toward the Lord and led him to betray Jesus (John 13:27). And, of course, there is the role the devil played in shaping Eve's attitude toward the Lord in the third chapter of Genesis.

Aside from spiritual influences, there are other influences we have to contend with as well. There is adversity, which according to scripture can have a positive or negative effect on attitude. There is the company we keep, again, positive or negative; there are also drugs (recreational, prescription, and illicit), which are even more of an issue today. Still, nothing has had a greater effect on our attitude at a personal level than our self-talk. Nothing affects the heart more than the endless dialogue we carry on with ourselves. Through our self-talk, we can create monsters or slay dragons. In James 3:13–18, the Lord's brother explains how all these forces work together to exert influence on our attitude.

In spite of all the negative influences we have to contend with, one thing has a positive influence on us that is greater than all the things I have mentioned, and that is love. It is the love of God poured into our hearts that gives us hope. It is the love of Christ that constrains us. It is the love we receive from God that shapes our attitude toward him and toward others. It is love that motivates our submission to the Lord's will and our investment in the lives of others.

Today, as you seek the Lord, ask Him to reveal the hidden areas of entitlement in your heart. Ask Him to show you the places where your opinion of *yourself* is too high or too low to handle life in a godly manner. Ask him to show you how to engage people out of your identity in Christ, not your self-esteem. Finally, ask the Lord to show you the situations and people (family, friends, coworkers, or vendors) with whom you need to change your approach. Meditate on the things that you would need to change if *you*—and not Christ—were the one Paul was using as the example in Philippians 2:1–11. Ask the Lord to make the changes in your heart that would make you a worthy example of a person with the proper attitude.

Day Seven

Courage

(Ephesians 6:10–20)

Today's topic of the heart is courage. Courage is the will to face our challenges with boldness even when it threatens our desires, exposure of your delusions or uncovers of your mask. It exists in the hearts of those who consistently choose reality over the fabricated world of fear. True courage is not the romanticized version of heroism frequently found in books and movies, where those who do not have an ounce of fear in them perform acts of bravery. Instead, it is a committed effort to live an authentic life, no matter the consequences.

The true nobility of a courageous heart is not the ability to vanquish fear; it is the commitment to embrace truth in all its forms with sobriety and vulnerability. For the courageous, the home of the brave is authentic expression, because they know the only place truly heroic actions can take place are in reality. Though worry and anxiety is a form of acknowledgment, they are not heroic, since none of the thoughts or decisions of the worried and anxious occur in reality; they take place in a fabricated world we imagine exist.

In Ephesians 6, Paul challenges the Ephesians to embrace reality to the fullest when he enlightens them about the considerable impact spiritual activity has on the physical realm of this world. One of the seminal acts of courage occurs when believers begin to engage the Spirit realm. Taking a stand against the kingdom of darkness is a choice to answer the call of God at the highest level. Acknowledging the existence and activity of the prince of darkness is a level of truth the faint of heart rarely take on because it backs them into a corner that leaves them only one option: to declare the true depth and nature of their faith and belief in the supernatural and subject yourself to the possible ridicule of those who may label their faith as irrational or extreme.

Having a worldview that embraces the notion of spiritual forces exerting influence on the physical world takes courage we might not otherwise feel compelled to display. Once we acknowledge the reality of the spirit realm, we will also have to acknowledge the existence of good and evil, which raises the issue of whose side are you on in the struggle. Picking a side presents another challenge to the courageous: the question of engagement.

Once we choose a side in a conflict, we are no longer neutral observers or innocent bystanders. We are now combatants who have to address the issue of how to engage the conflict and at what level. The side you're on should not be a secret. We must be bold without being arrogant. Along the way, we will be challenged to display a courage that vacillates between the public defense of our personal convictions and the private struggle to engage in behavior that consistently honors those convictions. Walking in this level of courage and commitment in a spiritually based worldview presents a third challenge we must come to terms with in our hearts: the notion of a spiritual adversary who is out to get us. Facing the prospect of this truth forces us to think and act more decisively, knowing that any misstep on our part provides an opening for temptation and accusation to enter. It would be wise to heed Peter's warning in 1 Peter 5:8 to be sober minded because the enemy is like a lion stalking prey.

As you seek the Lord's heart today, ask Him to give you a greater desire to embrace reality rather than in your imagination. Ask Him to reveal the areas of your life where you trust your imagination more than the Lord's power. Ask Him to give you the faith to revisit the places in your life where you no longer take risks because you imagine that a bad outcome would be too devastating to survive. Spend some time meditating on the things that he has already helped you overcome. How do the things that God has already given you the victory over compare to the things you are facing now? Ask yourself, "if the Lord can handle my past, then why can't He handle my future?" Ask the Lord to show you the areas in your life where you have ignored the supernatural influence of the enemy and not chosen to put on the whole armor of the Lord (Ephesians 6:13–17). Then ask the Lord to build you up in those areas.

Notes: Days 1-7

Introduction: Days 8–14

Amidst all the smoke ruble, chaos and confusion of the 9/11 tragedy, people running in two directions. The trained (first responders) were running toward a burning building, while the untrained (everyone else) were running away from a burning building, away from danger. Because of the first responders' training, they were able to overcome the natural instinct to run away from fire. Overcoming our default drives and urges to seek the path of least resistance is at the heart of every training program, especially when there is the potential we may have to endure pain or suffer a loss. Facing pain and loss is a key factor in determining the difference between better and best, survival and success.

For the next seven days of our thirty days of spiritual detox, we will be dealing with sacrificial strengths. I call these spiritual disciplines sacrificial strengths because the only way to cultivate their development in the heart is by making actual sacrifices. To acquire strength in these areas, you will have to willingly give up one or more of your rights. Like the training that first responders receive, this involves gaining mastery over the instincts that prevent us from being heroic.

There are two traits all sacrificial strengths have in common. The first trait they share is the reality that there is no quick and easy way to acquire these strengths. Like everything else in life that has real value, there are no shortcuts to obtaining them. No matter how you slice it, the process is going to be messy and drawn out! Further compounding the certainty of the long term and often-messy nature of the process is the reality the modern heart has been raised in an atmosphere of instant gratification, shortcuts and easy solutions. Keep in mind: this week is the beginning of a process; the goal of this week is to recognize and accept the costs associated with disciplining the heart. Nothing we look at this week will be resolved in one day or in one week! Get comfortable with the idea that every heart topic we will look at this week will be with us for the rest of our lives. There is not an "I have arrived" point to any of them to strive for. Like a gardener tending to a lawn, they do not turn the grass green; they tend it to keep it green.

The second thing all sacrificial strengths have in common is the effect they will have on your thinking, particularly on your assessment of what is reasonable. In Romans 12:1, Paul instructs the Romans to come before the Lord with a heart that is willing to live sacrificially, which he says is their rational service to the Lord—not something they should question, but something they should embrace.

As you walk with the Lord in sacrifice, you will build spiritual stamina that will also transform your thinking. Making you a mentally tougher. According to several passages of scripture (Romans 5:3–5; 8:18; 2 Corinthians 4:17; Philippians 1:3–7; James 1:2–4), those who embrace the process will grow in the insight, discipline, and peace necessary to manage the pain and loss of pursuing intimacy with the Lord. All of these passages provide assurance that the believer will experience the power, grace, and mercy of the Lord, as well as the affirmation of God's love in his or her heart.

May the Lord abundantly bless your efforts this week as you continue to seek His will with all of your heart, soul, and strength!

Day Eight

Humility

(James 4:1–10; Philippians 2:1–11)

Today's topic of the heart is humility. Humility is the management of life from the vantage point of three interlocking resolutions: you have nothing to lose that's worth more than your salvation, nothing to hide that Christ did not die for, and nothing to prove that the resurrection of Christ did not settle. It grows out of the acceptance of our full humanity. Humility does not flow from a heart that is trying not to appear proud; it flows from the heart of those who hope is anchored in the God's sufficient grace. It is only found in the heart that understands what Paul meant when he shared this revelation after he had sought the Lord three times to heal him of a chronic condition: "power is perfected in weakness" (2 Corinthians 12:9). The weaknesses that Paul is referring to in this passage are the imperfections, shortcomings and flaws we embrace about ourselves rather than cover with pride. God perfects human weakness by the power of His grace when we are authentic with Him and others about our inadequacies (James 4:7-10, 5:16).

Humility therefore is maintained by the symmetry between an inner strength we have gained from God and the honor we have for others; it exists in the heart only where envy, shame, and lust are confronted (James 4:1–5). To stay free from the vanity and idolatry of our age, we have to recognize and accept two things: the reality that our identity comes from God (Genesis 1:26; cf. 9:6; Romans 6:5–6; 1 Corinthians 15:49), and that God is the one who ultimately meets all of our needs (Genesis 1:29; cf. James 1:16–18). When these two things have been reconciled in the heart of the believer, humility flows from the heart and removes the need to defend, compare, or compete. Since self-worth comes from God and He is the one who meets our needs, we are able to honor others without a loss of dignity. Through our honor and acceptance of the core humanity of others and ourselves, we begin to take on the mindset of Christ as described in Philippians 2:1–11.

The real blessing of humility is that it allows everyone's needs to be met while at the same time preserving everyone's dignity in a way that is neither traumatic nor provocative. The bottom line is that humility removes the pressure of relating to one another by eliminating the competition and the defensiveness that is such a huge part of the way we do relationships now.

Walking in humility requires a working knowledge of the Lord's grace (James 4:6–10). It so easily moves from the heart to the head that we have to constantly expose our hearts to the truth; otherwise, it will turn into false humility. Of all the sacrificial strengths we will explore, humility is the one virtue that when cultivated will lead to the cultivation of the others. Among the various attitudes mentioned, humility is right there at the top of the list. In fact, you might call it the apex (highest) attitude because it is the one attribute found on every list of attitudes the Lord calls us to have (Deuteronomy 8:2-3,16; 2 Chronicles 7:14; Psalms 25:9; Proverbs 3:34; Philippians 2:5-8; 1Peter 1:5).

As you seek the Lord's heart today, ask Him to search your heart for any places where humility has indeed moved from your heart to your head. Ask Him to open your eyes to any area of your life where you feel the need to protect, hide, or justify your humanity. Identify the people that you are prone to doing these things with and ask yourself if these people have anything in common. Notice whether or not they are all authority figures, peers, etc.

If you find a particular group who you seem to have a pattern of relating to in this way, ask the Lord to show you where your confidence in yourself is out of balance with your honor for others. Confess any pride or idolatry that may be driving you to act in this manner. Meditate on the contrast between the roles that jealousy and humility play in *the acquisition of wisdom* according to James 3:13–18. Finally, ask the Lord to identify the area(s) in your life where your gifts and talents have bred pride and entitlement (a presumption of rights). Now, bring those rights before the Lord and offer them up as a sacrifice unto him.

Day Nine

Obedience

(Matthew 7:21–23; 1 Samuel 15:22–23)

Today's topic of the heart is obedience. Obedience is a commitment to follow the rules because you are following the Ruler. Consider the fact that the only difference between the words *obedience* and *audience* is *the prefix*. Both *obedience* (from the Latin *ob* meaning "toward" and *audire* meaning "hear") and *audience* (from the Latin *audientia,* present participle of *audire*) express the general notion of *giving someone your attention.* The notion that obedience involves hearing or listening underscores the relational dimension of obedience. When obedience is defined exclusively as "the keeping of rules," there is the risk for obedience to devolve into compliant rebellion. *Compliant rebellion* is cultivated in an atmosphere where we place the emphasis on rules and rituals rather than on our relationship with God. In hearts where compliant rebellion resides, people extend cooperation to the Lord without the requisite affiliation. They can be cooperative without consent.

In Matthew 7:21–23, Christ addresses the issue of compliant rebellion when He points out that not everyone who calls him Lord will enter into heaven, even if they have prophesied, cast out demons, and performed mighty works in His name. The reason He offers for rejecting them is that he never *knew* them. So even though they did the work in the Lord's name, the Lord still considers it an act of lawlessness, not because any of the works they performed violated a specific law of God, but because they did it without an established relationship to the lawgiver. It seems the real sin they were guilty of having was not violating the law; it was trying to relate to the law without relating to the lawgiver. Obedience is less about learning to follow the commands and precepts of the Lord, but is more about learning to relate to Him.

In the previous chapter of Matthew (6), Christ makes a similar assertion about the connection between devotion to the Lord and serving the Lord when He says that no one can serve two masters without developing a preference for one over the other—that will produce greater obedience for one than the other (see Matthew 6:24). King Saul also ran into the same problem when he tried to appease the people and please the Lord at the same time. In 1 Samuel 15:20–21, 24, King Saul admits he tried to appease the people and do God's will at the same time. In response to King Saul's explanation for not obeying the Lord, the prophet Samuel tells him his lack of devotion was tantamount to the practice of witchcraft and idolatry. At the end of their conversation, Samuel informed King Saul that the Lord tore the kingdom of Israel from his hands and gave it to the yet to be identified King David (a man after God's own heart).

As you seek the Lord's heart today, ask Him to show you the places where you have practiced compliant rebellion. Ask Him to show you the times when you were appropriate but not loving. Petition the Lord to show you ways that your heart can stay engaged in doing His will. Meditate on the cost of compliant rebellion based on Matthew 7:21–23 and 1 Samuel 15:22–23. Finally, consider the rights that you will need to give up—walking in obedience—by bringing those rights to Him. Offer them up as a sacrifice.

Day Ten

Grief

(Ecclesiastes 3:1–15; Philippians 3:1–14)

Today's topic of the heart is grief. Grief is the process we use to come to psychological terms with the autonomy of God and our dependence on God and others. Though grieving is very painful, it is always better than the alternative, which is getting stuck. The grief process is triggered by any loss that removes someone or something we've come to depend on so deeply (parent, spouse, job, health, child, etc.) that it challenges one of our major assumptions about reality (e.g., bad things should not happen to good people; or, playing by the rules always yields fair results).

Grief work is one of the truly difficult tasks we have to perform. Even though Ecclesiastes 3 makes it abundantly clear that grief is a natural part of the life cycle, most of us are not trying to hear that. One reason is because it is so painful and another is because it is a *process*, which in our culture are the two things we've been enculturated to resist. We are a nation in search of experiences without having to go through the processes. Instead of going through the process of putting the work in, we search for things like the NASCAR experience, fighter pilot for a day, pro baseball experience, and yes, the monastic weekend experience to feel what it is like to do something without having to pay the cost of actually having to apply discipline. Though loss is number one on the list of inevitable occurrences to take place in our lives, it also sits a top the list of things we are least prepared to handle when you consider the time, energy, and resources we spend trying to avoid any kind of loss.

There are a wide variety of ways unresolved grief can strike. It can suddenly and violently come upon you, or it can lie dormant just beneath the surface of your conscious awareness, for decades, possibly affecting every aspect of your life without you even knowing it.

Despite our negative attitude about grief, it is an awesome tool in the hand of a Holy God. Christ used grief to save our souls (Luke 22:39–46). Paul used it to pursue God's will for his life when explained he had suffered the lost of everything pursuit of his calling (Philippians 3:1–14). He also used it to prepare Timothy for ministry (2 Timothy). Job used grief to fend off discouragement when he told his wife, "the Lord gives and the Lord takes" (Job 2:9–10). John the Baptist used it to keep his ego in check when he said he must decrease as Christ increased (John 3:26–30). When we are willing to face our grief, the Lord can and will do great things in and through us. In Ecclesiastes 3:1, King Solomon declares there is a season for everything under the sun. Following that, he gives a rather exhaustive number of examples of seasons that occur in life. Remarkably, King Solomon's list contains several seasons God uses to grow our faith that require us to go through some sort of loss. Even in the sinless perfection of the Garden of Eden God established the role grief would play in the execution of His plan for humanity when He said: "Therefore shall a man leave his father and mother, and shall cleave unto his wife" (Genesis 2:24 KJV).

As you seek the Lord's heart today, ask Him to show you the areas where you have unresolved grief due to denial or avoidance. Ask the Lord to help you resolve these issues by strengthening you with His grace. Set aside some time today to meditate on the sovereignty of God and the limitation of your own humanity. Ask God to show you the places where you are living in the *delusion of control and prevention*. Finally, ask God to show you the times or seasons in your life when you felt like the Lord had not been fair to you (denied you one of your rights). Bring those grievances before the Lord and sacrifice them unto Him.

Day Eleven

Mercy

(Matthew 5:7; Galatians 6:1–4)

Today's topic of the heart is mercy. Mercy is the granting of another chance to someone who is, by all rights, out of chances. It is granted on the core belief that the greatest manifestations of human corruption can only be fixed by the greatest manifestation of the Lord's virtue, His mercy. Mercy covers the weaknesses in others with compassion, not denial. It is a choice to seek the best for others while they are at their worst.

One thing that makes mercy so difficult to extend is the way it is tied to the character of the person extending it. When the Lord extends mercy, He does so out of His character, never out of His assessment of the one who is in need of mercy. Ephesians 2:4 describes the Lord as being rich in mercy. Deuteronomy 4:31 describes the Lord as a merciful God. And in Lamentations 3:22–23, the writer tells us that God's mercy never ends; it is new every morning. From Genesis to Revelations the only source for God's mercy given is – His character, which for God is at all times righteous.

Unfortunately this is not the case for us. Our righteousness exists on a continuum that tends to decrease when someone offends us, which is why it is impossible for us to extend mercy without first grieving the offense.

Since mercy emanates from the character of the offended and not the offender, offering it forces us to face the ugly truth about others by facing the ugly truth about ourselves. It only springs forth from a heart that has been broken by an intimate knowledge of its own imperfections and capacity to wound. The immature heart that is still clinging to an offense cannot extend mercy. According to Galatians 6:1–4, one of the biggest challenges of walking with the spiritually fallen is not dealing with the sin that resides in the heart of the fallen, but dealing with the hidden sin in our own hearts. Walking in brokenness fosters an attitude that enables us to maintain a merciful disposition.

Brokenness is the by-product of yesterday's topic of the heart, grief. We cannot extend mercy until we have processed the full depth of the offense. Wherever we extend griefless mercy, the compassion necessary to soften the offender's hardened heart is missing because the mercy we offer isn't authentic; it is a cover-up, and like most cover-ups, it is more costly than the offense. Consider this: a close friend does something that hurts you deeply. When it finally comes to light, you minimize what happened by telling your friend, "It is not a big deal; all is forgiven." Not only do you push the pain in your heart down, but your denial also robs your friend of an opportunity to grow, and it further loosens the bonds between the two of you.

When Adam and Eve sewed fig leaves on themselves back in the Garden of Eden, they were also minimizing what had happened between the two of them. Neither of them were willing to address their shame with brokenness because neither of them were willing to do the grief work necessary to get in touch with the level of disappointment both were carrying toward one another. Instead, they practiced a shallow form of mercy. That is, until God stepped in, and Adam confessed he was afraid, naked, and hiding (Genesis 3:11). Not long after that confession, he expressed his frustration: he blamed God for giving him the woman, and Eve for leading him astray.

Immediately following His interrogation of Adam and Eve, God demonstrates the true depth of their offense. He kills an animal for its skin to provide covering for them (Genesis 3:21). Later on in scripture, the writer of Hebrews 9:22 clarifies this event when he states that almost everything is cleansed by blood, and without the shedding of blood, the sin that separates us from God and one another cannot be dealt with. What this implies is that in God's system of justice, we cannot extend mercy without grief. Christ's horrific death on the cross opened a portal that allows us to glimpse the depth of our sin. At the same time, it allows us to glimpse the depth of God's love. The simple fact of the matter is that mercy given without grief short-circuits the empathy and compassion needed for mercy to produce the shared grief necessary for relationships to be truly reconciled. There is simply no way for people to know how much you love them if you are not willing to show them how much you have been hurt by them.

As you seek the Lord's heart today, ask him to reveal the situations in your life where mercy was needed, but you chose some other way to manage an offense. As God reveals those situations to you, ask yourself, "Am I still holding on to the pain?" Ask the Lord to show you why you won't accept the corruption in yourself or others. Meditate on the role that pride might be playing in your reluctance to let things go. Ask the Lord to show you if your anger is in any way driven by unrealistic expectations that you have not yet resolved. Identify the rights you treasure the most that you will have to give up in order to receive the blessings of the merciful (Matthew 5:7). Then bring those rights before the Lord and offer them as a sacrifice unto him.

Day Twelve

Contentment

(Ephesians 4:22; Philippians 4:10–13; 1 Timothy 6:6–12)

Today's topic of the heart is contentment. Contentment is the choice to live well with less than what your potential can acquire. It is based on the belief the heart needs boundaries placed on it, or it will never be satisfied. The reason our hearts need boundaries, according to Jeremiah 17:9–10, is our hearts are full of desperation and deceit that are impossible to detect. According to James, desire breeds desperation and deceit (James 4:1-9). Whenever we have a strong desire for something and we satisfy it, we tell ourselves that we are satisfying our desire. The truth is we are building a greater appetite for what we desire. Getting the things we want fuels desire—it doesn't extinguish it. At the conscious level, we tell ourselves that we are going after something we think will satisfy us, while the truth is that we are going after something that will drive us in the future (Romans 1).

The desperation and deceit of the heart described in Jeremiah 17 occurs in four phases that successively impairs judgment (see Romans 1:18–28). Phase one is the luxury phase, when our desires come and go without much notice. Phase two is the convenience phase. During the convenience phase, our desires begin to surface as a distinct preference. In phase three, the need phase, a desire moves from a preference to a felt necessity. At this point, we don't have a desire— the desire has us. In phase four, the obsession phase, the corruption and impairment of our judgment is complete. During the obsession phase, desire corrupts our minds. In this phase, all the things that Paul listed in Ephesians 4:17–19—vanity, denial, alienation, blindness (ignorance), callousness, uncleanness, and greed—are in full bloom.

To counter the suffocating effect of deceitful desires, Paul says the mind has to be renewed (Ephesians 4:23). The Spirit doesn't just zap us with renewal in the spirit of our minds; on the contrary, it only happens when we embrace a life that's simpler than the one we can have (1 Timothy 6:6). Engaging the heart at this level requires the crucifixion of the flesh, along with its passions (Galatians 5:24). We must nail to the cross every craving that does not submit to the Spirit, where it must remain until it dies, no matter how much fighting, pleading, negotiating, accusing, rationalizing, rehearsing, and resisting takes place within our hearts. This is the process the Lord ordained in order to deliver us from the unhealthy craving that Paul says pierces our souls with many pains (1 Timothy 6:2–12).

As you seek the Lord's heart today, ask Him to show you the areas of your life where there is excess. Spend some time meditating on the things you can cut back on or eliminate that would free up your time and resources to serve others. Ask the Lord to help you reestablish your priorities. Make a list of things you currently want that you are going to choose to live without because of the potential to become a distraction (e.g., golf). Take note of things in your life that have changed priority: from a luxury to a convenience, from a convenience to a need, from a need to an addiction, and finally from an addiction to an obsession (e.g., a smartphone). Ask the Lord to show you the resources, privileges, and other things you have acquired that He may need you to give up. Then offer those things up to the Lord as a sacrifice.

Day Thirteen

Commitment

(Genesis through Revelation; Joshua 24:14–25)

Today's topic of the heart is commitment. Commitment, as I define it, is a skill set, not a desire, as some may define commitment. It is the ability to process your doubts about a person or situation with the person closest to the situation—while remaining engaged and accountable to the person while things are worked out. I know this is a mouthful, but every element of this definition identifies an important element of commitment.

Identifying commitment as an *ability* takes the concept of commitment out of the vague realm of feelings and circumstances. When I discuss commitment with people, they often talk about it as if it's a natural phenomenon that occurs when things between them and another are all lined up, like an eclipse. From their perspective, commitment is present when things are hard but not too hard, when others have gotten on their nerves but not their last nerve, or when they are frustrated but not burned out. Handled from this perspective, a situation that fades or worsens to a point we now find intolerable justifies the modification or abandonment of obligations we have toward a person.

Real commitment is *not* something that comes and goes with circumstances and feelings; it is an amalgam of skills that none of us are born with but that must be developed. There are three disciplines that you need to focus on to become a committed person: processing your doubts with the person you are committed to, remaining engaged with the person you are committed to, and accountable to the person you are committed to. We neglect and break commitments when we do not perform one of these disciplines. Sometimes, a person may withhold accountability because they have doubts and want to protect themselves from overinvesting in a relationship that may not last or that changes. Or they may stay engaged and accountable but process their doubts in secret. Are you getting the picture? Take away any element of commitment, and you no longer have commitment.

As you seek the Lord's heart today, ask Him to show you which of the three elements of commitment you struggle with the most. Ask the Lord to show you why this particular area of commitment is so difficult for you to manage. Identify the core concerns or fears you may have associated with your struggle, and then bring these before the Lord and ask Him to give you faith to confront these areas in your life. Meditate on the price that processing your doubts without communicating what is on your heart has cost you. Identify some of the ways your relationships would change if you walked in commitment according to the definition given. Finally, consider the rights you'll have to give up to protect the rights of the person to whom you are committed. Now bring those rights to the Lord and offer them up as a sacrifice unto Him.

Day Fourteen

Rest

(Ecclesiastes 2:15–26)

Today's topic of the heart focuses on rest. Rest is a physical manifestation of the acknowledgment of our frailties and God's sovereignty. When we consistently make getting the rest we need a priority, we affirm our faith in God and His faithfulness toward us. Resting the mind, body, and soul is an act of devotion that declares our faith in God's tenderness toward us as the provider of all our needs. When we resist the social norms that encourage us to push ourselves beyond the point of exhaustion, it is an expression of our confidence in God's power and provision! Taking time off without fear or anxiety about your career or the compulsion to amass more stuff requires just as much faith as trusting God for what you need.

Getting rest affirms our need for refreshing and renewal, which counters our tendency toward self-sufficiency. Rest transforms us from sprinters to marathoners. Those who value rest understand the importance of living to fight another day. Rested people tend to have fewer mood swings and a better attitude because periodic rest provides them with an opportunity to engage in reflection.

There is no sin the modern heart commits with more frequency and delusional pride than that manifested in our work-yourself-to-death approach to life and leisure. To understand how bad things have gotten, all you have to do is compare the architecture of the parks built today to those built over thirty years ago. There is a noticeable difference in acreage dedicated to vegetation, which promotes the enjoyment and relaxation of nature's beauty. A majority of the anchorage in the modern park is dedicated to competitive activity (baseball, soccer, football, etc.), which often features extremely bright lights for nighttime competitions and trails devoted to fitness rather than leisure or the observation of nature. Now, contrast the use of real estate today with that of parks built in the 1950s, '60s, and '70s—the lighting design and the space dedicated to relaxation and fellowship (trees, picnic areas, nature paths, etc.). Of course, when it comes to lighting in parks, safety is a definite concern. However, as shown in the 2007 documentary *Seeing in the Dark* and elsewhere, many of these ultra-bright lights waste energy, disrupt nocturnal cycles of plants and wildlife, and keep us from seeing the wonders of the night sky—God-given gifts we were meant to appreciate during leisure hours.

As you come before the Lord in prayer today, ask Him to show you the labors and activities you regularly engage in whereby you neglect your need for rest and renewal. Ask Him to show you the effect that fatigue is having on not only your performance, but on your *relationships* as well. Spend some time meditating on the unique ways you manifest frustration when you have pushed yourself too hard. Take time during your moments of prayer to just sit still before the Lord and rest in Him. Plan thirty minutes (or more) into your schedule to find a restful spot and do nothing: no cell phone, no work, no striving—nothing—just rest! After you finish, take note of how long it took your mind to settle itself, if at all. How hard was it to find a spot to do this? Did you feel any guilt, pressure, shame, or anxiety? If so, bring that before the Lord and ask Him to transform your thoughts about the necessity and value of rest.

Notes: Days 8-14

Introduction: Days 15–21

When a heart becomes so diseased that it no longer can support life, both doctor and patient are left with one drastic option: a procedure called a heart transplant. Heart transplantation is a very serious surgical procedure performed only on those with no hope of survival without it. Simply put, the heart must be replaced or the patient will die.

When it comes to a heart transplant, doctors generally have two options. The first rarely used option involves the removal of the diseased organ and replacing it with a manmade, artificial heart. Doctors rarely use this option because it only extends a person's life briefly. For all practical purposes, it is a stopgap measure. The second, more commonly used procedure involves the removal of the diseased heart and replacing it with a healthy donor heart. When this procedure is successful, it not only saves the life of the recipient, but also improves the quality of his or her life.

Throughout scripture, the heart of man is depicted as so diseased that the only legitimate option for survival is to perform a procedure similar to heart transplantation. In the book of Ezekiel (chapters 11 and 36), the prophet tells the people of Israel that their hearts were so diseased that restoration of the quality of life the Lord had promised them, the Lord would have to do more than change their fortune— The Lord would have to change their hearts.

Coming to terms with the depth of transformation necessary to walk with a "disciplined heart" is one of the most difficult tasks we face as disciples. For the next seven days of our thirty days of spiritual detox, we will look at seven topics that deal with the underlying malignancy existing inside the unregenerate and undisciplined heart. The main things these topics of the heart have in common are the significant transformational effect they have on our hearts. *Transformational disciplines* are disciplines we engage in that have a transforming effect on our hearts, which, by extension, includes our lives. Like heart transplantation procedures, transformational disciplines facilitate change in our hearts that profoundly improves the quality of our lives.

A Word of Caution

When a person receives an organ transplant, one of the greatest dangers they face postoperatively is a phenomenon called *rejection*. Rejection occurs when the immune system attacks the new organ as a foreign invader, even at the risk of the overall survival of the individual. As you pursue the transformational disciplines found in these next seven days, be mindful that rejection is not just a physical reaction; it is also a *spiritual reaction*. In the book of John (chapter 3), Christ tells Nicodemus that not everyone is willing to receive transformation because they prefer darkness to light. When the disciples could not keep watch with Christ, the Lord said that the spirit was willing, but the flesh was weak (Matthew 26:40–41). Watch for signs of spiritual rejection!

Unlike old soldiers, old habits don't just fade away; they stay and fight to the bitter end. Hang in there and fight back! Resist the temptation to give up the ground you have gained over the past two weeks. Be encouraged in the Spirit and in the power of the Lord, and finish strong! And as you pursue transformation, may the Lord restore your strength in Him.

Day Fifteen

Sabbath Day of Reflection

(Deuteronomy 6:1–9)

Today the topic of the heart is reflection. Spend today in reflection and prayer over things that stood out to you in the past two weeks. Take time to pray for your friends and family members in spiritual detox with you.

Day Sixteen

Faith

(Hebrews 11:1–40; Proverbs 3:5)

Today's topic of the heart is faith. Faith is the acceptance of reality in a state of intangibility—that can only be substantiated by hopeful action. In other words, faith is belief in the reality of something that one cannot touch but that one nonetheless acts upon because of the hope one possesses that makes it real. Its principal transforming property is its ability to extend our vision beyond the limitations of our sight, past experiences, fears, and anxieties. When we walk by faith and not by natural sight, our convictions rather than our circumstances drive us. We filter every aspect of life through our convictions about the character of God and the call we believe He has placed on our lives. Instead of amplifying the challenge through doubt and worry, we focus on the character of God.

Hebrews 11 lists several examples of people who overcame the limitations and obstacles of their circumstances through the application of faith. In this chapter, the writer explains the profound effects faith has on the life of the believer. The most significant is its impact on our worldview. Instead of living a life limited by personal discovery, the believer has the option to live by the revelation of the Holy Spirit, whose job it is to lead us into all truth. People of faith believe in a God they can know who controls the world; thus they live beyond the limitations of their own understanding.

As people of faith, we live according to the exhortation found in Proverbs 3:5, which encourages us to trust in the Lord, who controls everything, and not to depend on our own limited understanding. Instead of focusing on our problems, we focus on God, relying on the character of God and not our analysis of our current circumstances. Our conviction about the character of God relieves any anxiety about the uncertainty of our situation.

Ultimately, our knowledge of God's love for us trumps our fear of the unknown. Through the hope in and conviction about the character of God being built up daily through reading scripture, prayer, meditation, and so on, our inner self is strengthened and renewed daily. With a heart fortified by faith in God to stay focused God steers our lives toward the fulfillment of His promises and our destiny.

As you seek the Lord's heart today, ask Him to show you the areas in your life where your faith needs to extend your vision beyond a simple inventory of your circumstances. Ask the Lord to give you enough revelation of His character to walk faithfully before Him. Ask the Lord to remove the obstacles that hinder your ability to pursue your destiny in the Lord. Confess the areas of your life where you are not walking in your vision because of fear. Ask the Lord to show you the relationships that leaven (affect in a negative way) your faith, as well as those relationships that leverage your faith. Meditate, and lovingly act on ways to limit access to those who leaven your faith while increasing access to those who leverage your faith.

Day Seventeen

Purity

(2 Timothy 2:14–26; 3:1–7)

Today's topic of the heart is purity. Purity is one of the major themes of the Bible because of its close association with holiness. In Romans 12:1–3, Paul identifies three things that need to happen to walk in purity. The first part of the strategy is to maximize the impact and influence the Lord has on your character through the development of an increased sensitivity to the work of the Holy Spirit. To accomplish this, Paul told the Romans to present themselves before the Lord in a manner that reflected their acceptance of the Lord's standards of holiness as reasonable. This meant the Romans had to minimize the impact and influence of the Roman culture on the development of their character. To do this, Paul charged them with the second strategy needed to walk in purity—to recognize and resist the pressure to adapt to the unholy norms of Roman culture. The third thing Paul says must happen to produce transformation is the renewal of our thoughts and assessments about the world and ourselves, to create an atmosphere where true communion could take place. With so much of our thinking corrupted by our culture, we have to change our perspective before we can change our reality.

The principal transforming effect purity has on the heart is the same effect purity has on the physical body: it keeps us from getting and passing on things that cause harm. On several occasions, Paul cautioned Timothy, his son in the ministry, not to engage in intimate contact with those who walked in impurity, and on one particular occasion, Paul goes so far as to tell young Timothy to "flee youthful lust" (2 Timothy 2:14–26). In the very next chapter, Paul tells Timothy to turn away from those who *pretend* to walk in purity and holiness because association with them would make it impossible to live in truth, which ultimately corrupts a person's faith.

As you seek the Lord's heart today, ask Him to show you the areas in your life where you don't hold a standard of purity; then, turn that area of your life over to the Lord. After you have engaged in the *30 Days of Spiritual Detox* process, research and meditate on the scriptures that govern your area of spiritual neglect, and pick one of those scriptures to memorize. In the meantime, meditate on scriptures you are already familiar with that might apply to this area of your life. Ask the Lord to *heighten* your sensitivity to the things that you encounter in your daily routine that have a counter effect on your purity.

Day Eighteen

Peace

(Philippians 4:7-10; Colossians 3:12-17)

Today's issue of the heart is peace. Peace occurs when the three concepts of time: past, present, and future are in symmetry with one another. We are at peace when our thoughts and feelings about the past, present, and future have a positive effect on one another. On the other hand, peace is disrupted when our thoughts and feelings about the past, present, and future negatively affect one another. For instance, the thoughts and feelings from the past may negatively influence our thoughts and feelings about today's opportunities. Likewise, the thoughts and feelings we have in our present situation may affect the thoughts and feelings we have about the future. Being at peace means we have resolved the issues of our past to the best of our current ability, we are reasonably content with our current opportunities and efforts, and we remain hopeful concerning the future.

The principal transforming element of peace is its ability to guard our hearts and minds from the emotions that cause us to sabotage or surrender our destiny. When we walk in peace, our thinking is focused and clear we are free to do life without baggage, regret or hesitation. Paul gives us a clue about walking in the peace of God in Philippians 4 when he, points out the peace of God is associated with the ability to manage loss rather than gain stuff. When the strong desire to gain things controls or drives thought life, we live in a state of anxiety marked by the fear of measuring up to others and ultimate disappointment. Like a wandering dog, we spend more time chasing the scent of what we think will make our lives better than we do enjoying life. The more things we live without, the less the trivial interferes with the time, energy and resources that could be devoted to the significant filling our lives with the things that really matter to us.

In Colossians 3, Paul identifies another element of the heart that promotes peace: gratitude. Gratitude is an attitude of appreciation. It promotes harmony with others because it does not operate in entitlement. When we live in entitlement rather than gratitude, the expectations we have of others, which they will never be able to meet, shapes our relationships.

As you seek the Lord's heart today, ask Him to show you which of the three areas of time (past, present, or future) you struggle with the most. Then bring that element of time before the Lord and ask Him to give you peace with it. Ask Him to replace the emotions that cause you to sabotage or surrender your peace with resolve, contentment, or hope. Meditate on Philippians 4:7–10 and Colossians 3:12–17. Ask the Lord to show you the places in your life where your complaints, unforgiveness, and lack of understanding overrule His peace. Ask Him to settle your heart—not your grievances.

Day Nineteen

Forgiveness

(Matthew 7:1–5; 18:21–35)

Today's topic of the heart is forgiveness. Forgiveness is the prioritization of the mutual over the personal and the long-term over the present. It is the other side of mercy. In our discussion about mercy, we learned that it was predicated of the character of the one who extended it. Forgiveness on the other hand is predicated on the character of the offender. Extending forgiveness is not about us coming to terms with our character; it is about us coming to terms with the character of the one who has offended us. Forgiveness occurs when we embrace the true character of those who have offended us without holding him or her to the standards and expectations we have decided they should uphold. In forgiveness we release those who have offended us from the condemnation we have held against them, solely based on our expectations of them and not a legit analysis of who they really are. Forgiveness is extended when our minds make the shift from judgmental orientation based on presuppositions about what "should be" to a more flexible mindset based on what "is."

When people hurt or offend us, we must answer two questions. The first is, "Am I going to choose my disappointment over my relationship?" When we choose to walk in unforgiveness, we place ourselves above our responsibility and commitment to the relationship; at this point, blind spots develop that breed hypocrisy (Matthew 7:1–5). The second question is, "Am I going to put my present pain ahead of our future with others?" Another consequence of walking in unforgiveness is the toll it takes on the future. Walking in unforgiveness is always a short-sided strategy. When we judge people's behavior, we establish the standard for them judging us: heavily scrutinized people tend to scrutinize those who scrutinize them—*just as heavily!* We can all think of politicians or preachers that mocked the downfall of others only to receive a double dose of their own medicine when they fell.

The principal transforming effect of forgiveness is the promotion an atmosphere of grace over judgment. Forgiveness keeps the issues of the relationship *inside the relationship,* where reconciliation can take place. Forgiveness transforms any relationship into a refuge; unforgiveness transforms the people inside the relationship into refugees.

As you seek the Lord's heart today, ask Him to show you the person you have walked in unforgiveness toward the longest. Ask Him to soften your heart toward that person. Then ask the Lord to show you the people whose forgiveness you need to seek. Spend some time today meditating on the depth and frequency of the Lord's forgiveness toward you, and ask Him to help you see others' offenses as He sees yours.

Day Twenty

Confession

(Genesis 3:7–12, 21; Psalm 32:1–5; 1 John 1:5–10)

Today's topic of the heart is confession. Confession focuses on retaining our dignity through the acknowledgment of our personal frailties. It is the opposite of denial, which is the refusal to acknowledge our humanity. Those who live in denial rely on a manufactured personality to conceal their authentic self at the same time it highlights their inadequacies. All of the effort it takes us to maintain the manufactured personality has the paradoxical effect of drawing our attention to our shortcomings.

When we withhold the true nature of who and what we are in favor of a manufactured personality, our sense of self becomes bonded to our weaknesses. The application of our weaknesses, caused by living with the lives we show but are never quite able to believe, produces a shame that is more than a feeling—it is a state of being. In Psalm 32, King David compares denial to the wasting away of bones (v. 3) that can only be relieved through confession (v. 5). Confession is not only the acknowledgment that we are sinners, but it is also the acknowledgment that despite our sin, we are still worthy of love. People who practice sincere confession of their weaknesses put themselves in the best possible position to be healed (James 5:16; 1 John 5:9).

The principal transforming effect of confession on the heart is the authenticity it builds into our character. Confession prevents us from lying to ourselves about who we are, what we have done, and the consequences of our actions. It helps set the table for grace and mercy. From the time Adam ate the forbidden fruit, he went into a spiral of shame that was not broken until the Lord called him out (Genesis 3:7–12). Through the painful but necessary process of confession, Adam came to terms with himself, his sin, the love of the Lord, and ultimately the healing process. Once Adam confessed his condition, he stopped walking in denial and shame. Confession not only removed the burden of living a lie, it also exposed him to grace and mercy (Genesis 3:21).

As you seek the Lord's heart today, ask Him to show you the places in your life where you are still living with the burden of the lies you must tell to cover your sin, and confess those sins before the Lord. Now, go a step further and ask the Lord to show you any area in your life where you refuse to confess your weaknesses to others out of fear or pride. Then confess the sin of fear and pride (Romans 14:23; Luke 12:4, 5). Now ask the Lord to give you the strength to acknowledge your weaknesses through confession. Specifically ask for grace in these areas; spend time meditating on the liberty that confession brings to the soul.

Day Twenty-One

Worship

(Psalm 29:1–11; 96:1–13)

Today's topic of the heart is worship. Worship has had such a sweeping influence on human existence that it is impossible to give a succinct definition capable of doing the topic justice. The best anyone could do is to highlight a fraction of one element of worship. So, with that in mind, here is my definition of just one *aspect* of worship that I think is worthy of examination.

Worship is the authentic (from the heart) expression of awe that occurs when the all-knowing, all-powerful, ever-present Creator and Lord of the universe invades our reality, empties us of our vanity and pretense, fills us with his Spirit, and then replaces our vanity and pretense with affirming truth. It is the reverential amazement produced in our hearts when we meditate on three dynamics that define our relationship with God: the power of the Lord, the love of the Lord, and the frailty of our humanity. One of the more profound questions posed in scripture asks, "Who are we that an all-powerful God would love us so much?" (Psalm 8:4–9). When ancient cultures considered the question of the majesty of the Lord, his affection for humanity, and the frailty of man, *it produced an awe that defined worship!* But when modern man considers the same question, it produces shame because our culture has conditioned us to look at and be in awe of ourselves. Instead of responding to His affection, we respond to our defections. Genesis 3 tells us the first instinct Adam and Eve had when the Lord came to them after they sinned was to run and hide. One of the main culprits of our failure to worship is our preoccupation with our own deficiencies. When God confronts him, Adam makes a series of *I* statements—"I heard...I was afraid...I was naked...and I hid myself" (Genesis 3:10)—that indicate that even though he was aware of God, he was more aware of himself. What Adam displayed here is one of, if not the biggest hindrances to worship: the failure to recognize the coexistence of the awesome power of God and the awesome love of God.

When God asked Adam to divulge the source behind his sudden preoccupation with himself, he blamed Eve for giving him the fruit of knowledge of good and evil, even though it was not the source of his preoccupation with himself. The real source of Adam's new-found preoccupation with himself came from the behavior exhibited by him and Eve immediately after they ate the fruit–the judgmental comparing of themselves to one another, which led to an unhealthy obsession with themselves that escalated from covering their shame with leaves–to managing their shame by hiding among the trees. First Corinthians 10:12 clearly states that those who compare themselves with one another, whose standard of commendation is him- or herself, lack understanding. In verse 17, Paul identifies the real standard of commendation when he says that if anyone boasts, he or she should boast in the Lord, which is worship by definition.

The principal transforming effect of worship is its ability to frame our lives in a context of dependence on the Lord that accommodates our frailties and still glorifies God's character, particularly His power and love. Worship at this level is more than a sacrificial offering of praise to a worthy God, at this level worship elevates the human heart without usurping God's glory.

As you seek the Lord's heart today, meditate on the Lord's majesty and love, along with the things about yourself that He has exposed in the last three weeks. Then, instead of being ashamed of your humanity, focus on His majesty. Spend the day in worship, with the focus on Him rather than shame. Confess the areas of your life where the focus is on you being enough—not Him. Then surrender that area to the Lord.

Notes: Days 15-21

Introduction: Days 22–28

An arrhythmia is a medical condition marked by an irregular heart-beat. A person with an arrhythmia may have a heart that beats too fast (tachycardia), or too slow (bradycardia). Symptoms of an arrhythmia may be as benign as an unusual awareness of the beating of the heart (palpitations) or as potentially deadly as cardiac arrest, stroke, or embolism, which, if left untreated, can cause sudden death. In the late seventies, my mother had a cousin who lived in Arkansas who brought his family to California on vacation. During a trip to Universal Studios, he died suddenly from cardiac arrest brought on by a mistreated arrhythmia. I remember his wife telling my mother that he would not have died if his cardiologist had given him a pacemaker, a device placed in the chest or stomach to regulate the beat of the heart. It uses electric impulses to stimulate the heart to contract, controlling the heart's rhythm. When our natural pacemaker is unable to maintain a healthy heart rate, an artificial one is inserted to regulate the heart.

Regulation of the heart is an essential part of both a healthy physical and spiritual life. In the same way abnormal impulses can knock the natural heart's regulation out of sync, they can also knock the spiritual heart out of sync. Whenever we suffer emotional trauma, there is always the danger that we may develop negative impulses that will affect the regulation of our spiritual hearts. Over time, these impulses can damage our hearts; we may become depressed, bitter, defensive, fearful, or disillusioned until it becomes impossible to walk with the Lord or others. Like the person who has a heart arrhythmia, the spiritually traumatized are responding to potentially life-threatening impulses.

To counter this condition, we will spend the remainder of the thirty days of spiritual detox installing a "spiritual pacemaker." As our culture sinks deeper into narcissism and entitlement, it is becoming more difficult to love and honor the Lord and others. All of the remainder of the topics of the heart are designed to counter the carnal influences modern culture is having on our hearts. For the next nine days, we will explore the disciplines of the heart that function as spiritual pacemakers. Each of these topics of the heart functions in a way that they keep the heart in sync.

As you go through the nine days, be aware that these topics will expose you to a strategy that may leave you feeling vulnerable. Continue to maintain your consistency and zeal. Again, do not give back any ground that you have gained in the past twenty-one days. Press on until the Lord gives you total victory.

Day Twenty-Two

Resolve

(Daniel 1:8; 3:8–30; 6:14–24; Matthew 6:24)

Today's topic of the heart is resolve. Resolve is the wholehearted passionate pursuit of someone or something undergirded by a clear set of personal convictions. Convictions provide, the motivation to persevere, the peace of mind to remain focused and the resilience to overcome obstacles. It is a regret free decision to pursue something to conclusion *no matter what the cost.* People who have resolve derive their passion and focus from their personal convictions, which form the core of their identity, whether the circumstances are favorable or not. Produced by what is inside of us, resolve is commitment fueled by identity. When challenged, a person with resolve first asks, "Who am I?" and not "How bad is it?" or even "How bad do I want it?" Those who walk in resolve do not pursue goals they have set or solve problems when challenged; they pursue the strategy and path most consistent with their sense of self.

When viewed through the lens of circumstance, resolve is always vulnerable to change—no matter what the objective! Effective resolve, viewed through the lens of identity and not the variables of our circumstances, is stable. Resolve centered in our identity produces a higher degree of certitude and accuracy because it is *not* committing to an unknown variable; it is committing to a known variable, namely one's own character. The book of Daniel (1:8) states that Daniel "purposed" (resolved) in his heart that he would not defile himself with the king's provisions; Daniel's decision not to defile himself was based on his sense of identity as a Hebrew, not his circumstances as a slave. Even when he faced persecution, Daniel continued to walk in resolve (3:8–30; 6:14–24).

Wholehearted pursuit of anything requires the surrender of all competing loyalties and affections in the heart. In Matthew 6:24, the Lord said it was impossible for a person to serve two masters, because over time we will come to resent one and love the other. In the parable of the sower in Matthew 13:3–9, the Lord identified one of the major reasons why people are not productive: the presence of competing loyalties and affections. When our loyalties and affections compete with one another, they choke off the passion and energy necessary to produce tangible results. James 1 further tells us that a lack of resolve can hinder results.

As you seek the Lord's heart today, ask Him to reveal the places in your life where you have competing loyalties and affections. Ask Him to show you the effect your present circumstances are having on your productivity. Spend some time in meditation, focusing on the things you have to pursue with resolve because of who you are. Make a list of the your current priorities —that you would have to give up—if your priorities were driven by your identity and not your desires. Draw a line through the things on your list that you are willing to give up. Ask the Lord to incline your heart to make choices consistent with your identity—not your desires.

Day Twenty-Three

Love

(John 15:14; James 5:20; 1 Peter 4:8)

Today's topic of the heart is love. Love is the resolve to extend good-will to another person, despite his or her response to your goodwill. Because we use the word *resolve* to define love, love also draws its reason from *within.* A loving person never asks if the object of their affection is worthy of their love; instead, a loving person asks, "Have I given love at a level consistent with the type of lover I am?" One of the key presup-positions of love is the belief that the most effective way to deal with the countless ways we disappoint one another is to keep our hearts softened toward and engaged with one another (John 15:13–14). According to scripture, love covers a multitude of faults (James 5:20; 1 Peter 4:8) and casts out fear (1 John 4:18). Only a heart willing to encounter someone else—despite his or her shortcomings—can truly love. To maintain a soft heart, a person must be able to manage his or her own shame and desire without being provoked.

As you seek the Lord's heart today, ask Him to show you the rela-tionships where you have not resolved to extend goodwill. Ask Him to reveal unsettled desires and shame that still exist in your heart that prevent you from extending goodwill. Confess these things and ask the Lord to forgive you of these things and resolve them. Ask the Lord to show you the role your perception of a person's worth plays in how you treat them. Ask Him to soften your heart toward those from whom you have disengaged but with whom you need to reengage. Finally, ask Him to incline your heart to extend goodwill to people—even when they provoke you.

Day Twenty-Four

Submission

(John 17; Ephesians 5:15–21)

Today's topic of the heart is submission. Submission has two major components: recognition that the only healthy way to manage power is to share it and knowledge that the only way to share it is without ego. Sharing power without ego is one of the most consistent themes Christ taught, modeled, and prayed (John 17). Godly submission is rooted in the principle that all legitimate power comes from the Lord and is exercised through the consent to share it. It is never parasitic or predatorial.

As you seek the Lord's heart today, ask Him to show you the places where you refuse to either share power or you do so with your ego involved. Ask Him to build your understanding and appreciation for submission. Confess any rebellion or fear that hinders your relationships from reaching their maximum potential. Spend the day meditating on the difference between your definition of submission and the one presented here. Ask the Lord to incline your heart to walk in submission when necessary, which is anytime you are working with another person.

Day Twenty-Five

Grace

(2 Corinthians 12:7–10; James 1:5)

Today's topic of the heart is grace. Grace is the accommodation we make for the weaknesses of others. It allows them to struggle with the inconvenient truth of their lives, and at the same time preserve their dignity. According to John 1:16–17, Moses brought the Law into believers' lives to handle their weaknesses, while the Lord brought grace into believers' lives to manage the weaknesses in others. Using the Law to manage weaknesses meant the believer had to live with the fear of judgment. On the other hand, using grace to deal with the weaknesses of others eliminates the fear of judgment because it does not prescribe a standard of judgment the way the Law does; it prescribes a standard for our reaction when the Law is broken.

Paul summarized the effectiveness of grace, when shared the Lord's answer to a prayer he'd petitioned the Lord to answered on three separate occasions. Very simply the Lord told him: "*My grace is sufficient for you, for my power is made perfect in weakness*" (2 Corinthians 12:9, emphasis added). The point he was making was clear: grace covers human frailty without exposing the person unnecessarily. The book of James describes how this works when James (1:5) informs his readers that if they lacked wisdom, all they had to do was ask the Lord and He would give it to them generously without shaming them for their ignorance, which is simply a lack of knowledge that should carry no shame or guilt, unlike a lack of character.

When Noah got drunk after the flood and lay naked on his bed, it was his son Ham who saw and exploited his father's shameless exposure (Genesis 9:20–22). It was his other two sons, Shem and Japheth, who showed him grace when they acknowledged it by walking into their father's room backwards with garments and covering him (Genesis 9:23). What Shem and Japheth did was a textbook example of how grace works: they did not deny their father's shameless behavior, nor did they exploit it. Instead, they did whatever they could to address it without doing any further harm to their father's dignity.

As you seek the Lord's heart today, ask Him to show you the places in your life where you struggle with the efficacy of grace by demonstrating a preference for judgment. Ask Him to give you insight into the weaknesses that keep you from walking in grace; ask Him to reveal any area of pride in you that keeps you from acknowledging your need for grace. Spend the day meditating on the grace of the Lord. Ask the Lord to incline your heart to preserve the dignity of others in the same way Shem and Japheth did for Noah, even if it is not reciprocated.

Day Twenty-Six

Joy

(Psalm 100; Job 2:9–10; Philippians 4:11–12)

Today's issue of the heart is joy. Joy is deep satisfaction with life rooted in a worldview that believes God is both sovereign and good (Psalm 100). True joy is rooted solely in the character of God and not in fortune or luck (Psalm 5:11–12; 16; 30:4–5). One of the hallmarks of people who walk in joy is their ability to adjust their perspective to their current circumstances (Job 2:9–10; Philippians 4:11–12) in a manner that prevents them from ever seeing him or herself as a victim (Romans 5:3–5; 15:13; James 1:2–4). The joyful see life as a gift—not an entitlement. Their optimism is derived from a core conviction about the goodness of the Lord (Psalm 106:1; 147:7–11).

In the hands of a believer, joy is not just a state of consciousness; it is strength (Nehemiah 9:36) even when life is in shambles, because the true believer does not put trust in the prospect that his or her fortune will change. They know circumstance do not have to change for them to succeed because, they are mindful the Spirit of God has the transformative power to change their attitude, mood and perspective. Without changing their circumstances. The joyful are dependent on the love, power and providence of God, to see them through the trying times. In the midst of their trials they reflect on the providential care the Lord has shown them and others. Like King David, the joyful know how to encourage themselves in the Lord (1Samuel 30:6).

As you seek the Lord's heart today in prayer, ask Him to reveal the places in your life where you have no joy because you are stuck focusing on your circumstances, rather than on God's providential character. Ask the Lord to show you the places where you may need to encourage yourself. Spend some time meditating on the areas of your life where you have doubts about the goodness of the Lord. Confess those areas to the Lord, and ask Him to heal you of your doubt. Make a list of the providential acts God had to perform to preserve you to this day. Make sure you include some of the actions He had to take in previous generations. Ask the Lord to give you the wisdom to put your life and circumstances into *proper perspective*. Finally, ask Him to incline your heart to appreciate your life—rather than judge or question it.

Day Twenty-Seven

Honor

(Proverbs 27:18; Genesis 9:18–27;1 Samuel 24:1–9; 2 Samuel 15:1–12)

Today's topic of the heart is honor. Honor is the ability to respect the position of another despite his or her performance in their position without envy or resentment (Proverbs 27:18). Since there are no perfect leaders and no perfect followers, there is always the potential that the relationship between the two can become abusive. Normally when we think of an abusive relationship, we think of the misuse of power on the part of the leader. Yet the misuse of access to the powerful can be just as abusive on the part of the follower when they become too familiar. When tasked with the job of walking closely with a leader, you may be granted a level of access that exposes you to the leader's shortcomings, which over time you may be tempted to exploit.

Two things dwell in our hearts that may cause us to exploit our access to those in authority. The first is envy. As we take note of the failings of those in positions of authority and influence, we could easily conclude they are neither worthy nor qualified to fill their position, especially if we consider ourselves more qualified because of our résumés or character. The second thing that dwells in our hearts that may cause us to exploit our access is resentment. When resentment toward those who have authority over us settles in our hearts, our hearts become hardened. Once envy or resentment is present in the heart, rebellion is not far behind. Such rebellion may be as subtle as slanderous gossip or as overt as open challenge, which seeks to remove the leader from his or her position. In any case, it is just as abusive for the follower to abuse his or her access to those in power, as it is for the leader to abuse his or her power.

This is what happened when Miriam and Aaron spoke against their brother Moses for marrying a Cushite woman. In Numbers 12:1–2, they ask whether God has only spoken to Moses, noting that he has spoken through them as well. The issue they had with Moses is one that those tasked with walking intimately with leaders all struggle with: fusing their function with their value and therefore, their value with their position. What this inevitably leads to is greater scrutiny of the leader on the part of those close to the leader. To demonstrate how serious the Lord is about honor, he struck Miriam with a skin disease that Moses had to intercede on her behalf for her healing. (Numbers 12:3–16).

As you seek the Lord's heart today in prayer, ask the Lord to search your heart for the presence of envy or resentment toward anyone who holds a position of authority or influence in your life. Confess, repent, and release any resentment or envy you may have toward anyone. Meditate on the actions of Ham, Shem, and Japheth (Genesis 9:18–27), and ask the Lord to show you which son's behavior best represents your behavior toward your parents. Meditate on the actions of King David (1 Samuel 24:1–7) and his son Absalom (2 Samuel 15:1–7). Ask the Lord to show you which heart is closest to yours when you feel that those in authority have mistreated you. Ask the Lord to reveal any relationships in your life where a Miriam-and-Aaron attitude might be setting up in your heart. Finally, ask the Lord to incline your heart to honor rather than expose those who have authority over you.

Day Twenty-Eight

Authenticity

(John 4:7–45; 8:32; 14:15–17, 26; 15:26; 16:12–13; Psalm 51:6)

Today's topic of the heart is authenticity. Authenticity is living your life in a manner that corresponds to reality and not imagination, without judging yourself or having undue regard for the judgment of others. It combines the Latin prefix *aut-* (meaning "self") with the Greek word *hentes* (meaning "doer" or "being"). Placed side by side, this combination defines *authenticity* perfectly: doing or being you. To do and be who you really are, you must be willing to embrace the truth of who you are in a nonjudgmental manner that allows you to walk in freedom.

In the book of John (4:7–42), Christ demonstrates the liberty of walking in authenticity during a conversation with a Samaritan woman. In this conversation, Christ challenges her to embrace the truth about her many failed relationships. From the time she embraces the truth about her past, she is able to talk about it openly and publicly. What is striking about this encounter is the liberty that she is able to walk in, just by embracing the truth. At the conclusion of the conversation, Christ informs the woman that the Father (God) is looking for people who do truth, not religion. We see further evidence of the Lord's desire that we embrace truth in Psalm 51:6, where King David states that God is delighted with a heart filled with truth. In John 8:32, Christ tells new believers it is knowledge of the truth that will set them free. To underscore the Lord's desire to see us live authentic lives, He gave us the Holy Spirit to guide us in the discovery of the truth and to comfort us about the truth we discover (John 14:15–17, 26; 15:26; 16:12–13).

As you seek the Lord today in prayer, ask Him to show you the situations and circumstances in your life where you are more concerned about people's perception of you than you are in reality. Ask the Lord to show you the places where your unwillingness to embrace the truth is hindering your worship. Ask the Lord to show you a truth that he would like you to embrace that would please Him. Spend some time meditating on how a conversation with the Lord would go if John 4:7–42 were about you; what would you be free to talk about openly and publicly? Finally, ask the Lord to incline your heart to love truth and walk in authenticity.

Notes: Days 22-28

Summary: Days 29–30

One the most difficult aspects of treating heart patients involves their commitment to aftercare programs. Once a crisis has been averted and patients start to feel better, it is easy for them to slip back into old habits. Making follow-up appointments to monitor the heart's ongoing condition is essential. Failure to follow up with the aftercare portion of a treatment plan is one of the leading causes of fatal heart disease. Once again, we can apply the same principles to the spiritual heart.

Once the thirty days of spiritual detox are over, it is important that you do not slip back into old habits. Take some time to determine the next thing you are going to do to support the health of your spiritual heart. You may want to go back over some of the most challenging topics. You may want to spend as much as a week delving into each one. *Most importantly, decide on something. Do not let the thirty days just end and the momentum you have built up end with it.* You have made major progress over the past twenty-eight days. Think about it: for the last twenty-eight days, you have read your Word daily, spent consistent time meditating on scripture, and praying continually. I want to take this time to encourage you to continue to walk in the spiritual momentum you have generated when the thirty days are up.

Another thing I want to encourage you to do today is to designate a time no sooner than three months and no later than nine months from now to go back through *30 Days of Spiritual Detox*. The testimonies of the revelation received from the Lord that those who have gone through the detox more than once have reported are amazing.

Even though a typical detox program is twenty-eight days, or four weeks, this one is a full thirty days because it allows us an additional two days to summarize and review. For the next two days, we will examine two major themes of the spiritual detox that encompass every element of the issues of the heart we have looked at for the past twenty-eight days.

Day Twenty-Nine

Adaptability

(Days 1–28: Summary and Review)

Today's topic of the heart is adaptability. Adaptability is like commitment; it is a skillset. It is the ability to remain faithful through change and challenge. To manage change and challenge faithfully, time and effort must be spent training and developing the heart to engage every aspect of the human condition. In a constantly changing world, we spend the bulk of our time developing our technical rather than adaptive skills. From the time we discover we can do something well, we spend our time getting better at it. Far too much time is spent developing talent rather than developing the heart. An endless number of subcultures in the way of camps, leagues, federations, associations, private lessons, media, seminars, and tournaments are available, devoted to the development of talents in every conceivable endeavor, without ever attending to the development of the heart. We fine-tune every aspect of our performance except for how the heart will hold up under the social pressures associated with performing under changing conditions. For example, we may spend a decade or more preparing professional athletes to play but no time preparing them to handle success or life when they have to walk away from the sport. The average parents spend years preparing their child to go off to college, but never give one thought to preparing that same child for the routine of coming home to a spouse daily. Developing a heart to manage an ever-changing world starts to address any delusions we have about the level of control we have over our environment, along with any delusions we have about our power to prevent things from happening. The goal of this process is to foster faithfulness, not perfection. Perfection requires perfect responses to perfect conditions. Faithfulness requires an enduring response under any condition. Faithfulness is not about the environmental conditions we face; it's about the condition of the heart. At the conclusion of Hebrews chapter 11, also known as the faith chapter, the writer talks about a multitude of believers who he commended for their faith but who nevertheless died not receiving what was promised (Hebrews 11:39–40). The reason the writer commended their faith was that faithfulness is not about producing results; it is about maintaining hope no matter how many twists and turns life throws at us. This was the sentiment expressed by King David when his child, who was the product of an affair, fell sick and died (2 Samuel 12:14–23). When asked by his servant how he could fast and pray for his child to be spared and then rise up and praise God when those prayers went unanswered, King David answered by saying, "While the child was alive, I prayed not knowing if God would answer my prayer. When the child died, why should I continue to focus on something that is over that I can no longer fix?" While King David's son was alive, he met the requirement of faithfulness by fasting and praying for his son. When the child died, King David met the requirement for faithfulness by rising up and going to the house of the Lord to worship. In both instances, King David adapted to the changing demands of his situation with faithfulness.

As you seek the Lord in prayer today, ask Him to show you which of the first twenty-eight topics you need to work on the most to take your faithfulness to another level. Ask Him to show you the areas of your life where your technical skills do not match your adaptive skills. Meditate on the effect change has on any of the topics we have covered over the last twenty-eight days. Finally, ask God to incline your heart to embrace change as a chance to seize new opportunities.

Day Thirty

Sobriety

(Days 1–28: Summary and Review)

The final topic of the heart is sobriety. Sobriety is a multifaceted word that directly and indirectly covers all the topics of the first twenty-eight days. Sobriety is the exercise of good judgment in spite of your desires or distractions. Living a sober life is living your life with *a clear set of boundaries*. Boundaries are dividing lines that mark where something ends and something else begins.

Discerning the beginning and ending points of something is the essence of good judgment, one of the subtexts of *30 Days of Spiritual Detox*. When the apostle Paul exhorts the saints at Rome not to think more highly of themselves than they ought (Romans 12:3), he is shining a spotlight on the ultimate danger of poor judgment and the greatest challenge to spiritual health and maturity: self-deception. Self-deception occurs under one of two conditions. The first potential situation where self-deception can occur in our hearts when we become so toxically burdened by our gifts, talents, goals, need for achievement or affirmation that we are too overwhelmed to recognize and accept our need for God's grace. The second potential situation where self-deception can occur in our hearts when we become so toxically dependent on our gifts, talents, goals, and achievements that we no longer walk in faith.

Managing the specific burden of our call without being over-whelmed and managing the success of walking in our call without being seduced into believing we have arrived are the two greatest threats to walking in sobriety. Being burned out or turned out are two conditions that contribute most to the hardening of our hearts toward God, and the subsequent decision on our part to walk by sight and not by faith (Romans 1:5,18–32).

To guard the heart against slipping into self-deception, Paul does not issue a command to obey or steps to follow. Instead, he encourages believers out of the grace he has received to "think with sober judgment, each according to the measure of faith that God has assigned" (Romans 12:3). His exhortation to think and live in a sober-minded way—marked by unhurried thoughtfulness, without the extremes of impulse or prejudice—is not some cookie-cutter principle that fits everyone the same way. On the contrary, it is a subjective self-estimate that requires discrimination and discernment guided by the hand of God in your life. Here Paul is challenging us to walk in the shoes of his forefather, King David, and open ourselves up to the need to have our hearts searched continually, which brings us full circle (Psalm 7:8–9; 11:5; 26:2; 139).

As you seek the Lord in prayer today, spend time meditating on the progress you have made in the past thirty days, or however long your undertaking has been with this book. Spend time in thanksgiving and praise for the spiritual progress you have made and the intimacy with the Lord you have experienced. Ask the Lord to nurture what He has deposited in you. Pray that He would give you revelation about the doors that this process has opened, so that you may now step through.

Finally, it is important to recognize this as the beginning of something, and not the end. Spending time in detox is not the end of the party; it is the beginning of your spiritual sobriety. Embrace your spiritual sobriety—you have put the work in!

Notes: Final Take Aways

Acknowledgments

Because meaning is delineated by the quality of our relationships and not individual achievement I would like to acknowledge the following people: the entire Covenant Blessing Family members and staff, past and present, for their encouragement and support over the past thirteen years. I would also like to thank my covenant mothers for their unique contribution to the refinement and publication of this project. Special thanks also goes out to C. Jeff Wright and Ted Alston for their counsel, Melanie and Monica Austin for their tag team work in getting this project completed and Falana Monroe for reigniting my passion for writing – "It's not complicated it's just scary."